UNICORN

Make the Move

Demystifying Entrepreneurship

Ishan Gupta, Rajat Khare

Publishers
UNICORN BOOKS, New Delhi-110002
E-mail: unicornbooks@vsnl.com
Website: www.unicornbooks.in • www.kidscorner.in

Distributors
Pustak Mahal, Delhi
J-3/16, Daryaganj, New Delhi-110002
☎ 23276539, 23272783, 23272784 • *Fax:* 011-23260518
E-mail: info@pustakmahal.com • *Website:* www.pustakmahal.com

London Office
5, Roddell Court, Bath Road, Slough SL3 OQJ, England
E-mail: pustakmahaluk@pustakmahal.com

Sales Centre
10-B, Netaji Subhash Marg, Daryaganj, New Delhi-110002
☎ 23268292, 23268293, 23279900 • *Fax:* 011-23280567
E-mail: rapidexdelhi@indiatimes.com

Branch Offices
Bangalore: ☎ 22234025
E-mail: pmblr@sancharnet.in • pustak@sancharnet.in
Mumbai: ☎ 22010941
E-mail: rapidex@bom5.vsnl.net.in
Patna: ☎ 3294193 • *Telefax:* 0612-2302719
E-mail: rapidexptn@rediffmail.com
Hyderabad: *Telefax:* 040-24737290
E-mail: pustakmahalhyd@yahoo.co.in

US$ 10, UK £ 6, Euro • 8

Website: www.makethemovebook.com.
E-mail: info@makethemovebook.com.

ISBN 978-81-7806-114-6

Edition : 2007

Printed at : Pushp Print Service, Delhi

Dedication

This book is dedicated to all those who form an integral part of our lives. An enormous thanks to our parents and grandparents who have always put their trust, believed in us and encouraged us throughout. Thanks a lot to all our friends whom we've met at different stages in life including big bro Anuj, Tarun, Bhavna, Divya, Kirti, Vipin, Nikhil, Ankur(s), Jitin, Narendra, Saurabh, Mayank, Aman, Varun(s) and Khushboo who have always been there to help us make the move.

A very special thanks to Divya Laul whose immense hard work has gone into taking the writings from both of us and combining them into one single work, and then editing it. Thank you Arnav Bhavya for the very creative cover page, Neha for the wonderful cartoons and Anuradha for providing us with classified information from time to time. We would like to thank the team at Unicorn Books for the support they gave to us at every step.

This book would not have been complete without the love and affection showered on us by all our special co-authors who took out time from their busy schedules to meet, share their values and write for us. We really appreciate all of them for their passionate words of encouragement.

Last but not the least, we would like to thank you, the reader who now holds this book, We would love to hear from you at info@makethemovebook.com. We hope you will also, Make The Move!

Contents

Foreword *07*

Part - I

1. Re-defining Entrepreneur and Entrepreneurship 13
2. Essentials of Entrepreneurship 19
3. Initial Phase of Entrepreneurship 27
4. Understanding Finance 34
5. Conversion to Serious Business 51
6. Scaling the Business – "Realising the Vision" 56
7. Human Resource Management 63
8. Marketing Expertise 67
9. Brand Development and Management 80

Part - II

Our Own Story 91
(December 23rd 2003, 9:15 p.m.)

Part - III

❖ Those who 'Made the 'Move' ❖

Experience Cannot be Taught 101
(Ambika Pillai)

Entrepreneurship is the Way to Live 103
(Anuj Khare)

Follow Your Instincts 107
(Arjun Malhotra)

The Fashion Guru 110
(Ashish Soni)

Dance from the Heart 113
(Ashley Lobo)

Challenges for the Entrepreneur 118
(Dilip Cherian)

Obsessive Passion 120
(Dilip Chhabria)

Gaining A Winning Edge 123
(Dr. Kiran Mazumdar-Shaw)

Globalising a Legacy 125
(Mohit Burman)

Escorts Towards Newer Horizons 129
(Nikhil Nanda)

Entrepreneurs and Entrepreneurship 132
(Prof. Patrick Turner)

Yes, You Can Do It! 137
(Pradeep Chopra)

Spreading the Technology Information 144
(Pradeep Gupta)

Creating a Groundswell of Computer Professionals 148
(Rajendra S. Pawar)

Dare to Dream, Dare to Fail, Dare to Resurrect, Dare to Succeed 151
(Raveena Raj Kohli)

Putting your Money Where your Mouth is 152
(Sandeep Tyagi)

Entrepreneurship in the Internet Era 154
(Tarun Wig)

Sharp Focus is a Must 157
(Vishnu R. Dusad)

Foreword

"The greatest risk in life is not to take one at all."

When Ishan and Rajat asked me to write the foreword for "Make The Move", the fire and passion that I saw in their eyes got me thinking about why entrepreneurship attracted me in the first place and what aspect of my own entrepreneurial adventures I could share with readers of this book.

The answers to both these questions, as it turned out, were quite straightforward! There is a widely-held misconception that being an entrepreneur is about taking big risks with a singular goal of hitting a jackpot payoff – a Russian roulette-style high risk, high reward game. Entrepreneurship is not only about money – which, if anything, should be a byproduct and not a goal in itself. The more exciting aspect is the thrill of the chase – the promise of taking a thought germinating in your mind and growing it in the real world into an entity that provides value on some dimension to millions of people. Also, while being an entrepreneur carries a lot more risk than the average 9-to-5 job, a smart entrepreneur knows how to de-risk himself to the fullest extent possible and keep things going through bad times. There is always the risk that things will not always go as per plan and there will always be mountains to climb but if the battle is worth fighting, these are nothing more than minor niggles which make the taste of victory that much sweeter!

From my own experiences as an entrepreneur, I believe there are four factors essential for success. The first and most important one is the team. No matter how good an idea you have, or how big a market you're going after, you will not succeed unless you have the right team. Putting the right team together is more a matter of chemistry than arithmetic. If the members in a team do not enjoy working with one another and value the contributions of each other, success is a remote possibility. Having a motivated group of people enhances work experience by leaps and bounds and makes the entrepreneurial journey all the more enjoyable.

The second element is having a handle on execution risk. Do you have the wherewithal in terms of knowledge, time, finances and resources to take your idea to fruition? While it might seem very attractive to take on a major challenge at the first pass and aim for the moon, temper your goals by matching these goals to your ability to execute – this will teach you to focus on the fundamentals and apply your resources to tackle those problems where you have your core strengths.

The third factor is the financing risk. You will need to ensure that you have enough money to take your idea through to completion. Remember the adage that goes – "Cash flow is king"!

The last factor is the market risk. Once you've created something, will the market consume it? You may think it's a good idea, but the market is the ultimate test both in terms of end-users seeing value in your offerings and competitors not being able to offer similar or superior solutions. Make sure that you validate the value of your offering in the product as soon as possible in the company life cycle. Use the feedback to build out your product roadmap and iteratively improve your offering.

The Internet has opened up tremendous opportunities for individuals to make a mark. One remarkable aspect of the Internet is that it levels the playing field to the extent that a small start-up can compete on equal footing with large established behemoths, provided its offering is innovative and compelling enough. My own case, Hotmail, is a great example of how two engineers with no prior experience and backing could build out an offering that attracted millions of users while other companies spending millions of dollars on development and advertising could not attract such large user bases. I believe the time is now ripe for creating many such Hotmails right here in India.

In India, the stigma of failure is a powerful driver and it requires individuals with a great sense of destiny and unbridled faith in their own abilities and vision to succeed. People constantly ask me why I haven't "retired" after earning a fortune with Hotmail, and why I am taking the risk of nurturing new ideas through my companies like InstaColl and Blogeverywhere, where I run the risk of getting stigmatised if they fail. The answer to this is in the first line of this foreword. It is now my burning desire to see a "Made in India" product company succeed in the same way that Hotmail did in the US and that is the reason why I continue to be an entrepreneur tilting at windmills against competitors with enormous resources.

We are living in interesting times. The progress that we can make, as individuals and as a nation, is only limited by our enthusiasm and our imagination.

The book will help to demystify the factors surrounding entrepreneurship for you and hopefully inspire you to start your own venture and follow your own dreams.

Go ahead and make the move – and rest assured that irrespective of to whatever extent you succeed, your entrepreneurial adventure will be the most exciting journey of your life!

—Sabeer Bhatia

Part - I

1

Re-defining Entrepreneur and Entrepreneurship

'Entrepreneur' is a word probably not very easy to spell. Ask just about anyone walking on the road to spell it and you will see that one or more 'e's and the 'u' will be missing from the spelling. Maybe there is a reason behind it. The reason is that not many people have started the journey of becoming an entrepreneur. It is a journey which is full of hard work and dedication. Learning the spelling is the least of your worries, because that's something an entrepreneur comes to know about when he decides to write a book!

Entrepreneurship is nothing but following your heart and soul and making an effort to fulfil your dreams. When you decide to start your own company, when you decide to become the next Arnold Schwarzenegger or Shah Rukh Khan, when you decide to become the next Miss India, when you decide to become the next Sachin Tendulkar or Muhammad Ali, you become an entrepreneur. Because at that very time, you consciously take your life and your destiny in your own hands and work at it to achieve your dream. And that's what entrepreneurship is all about. "Entrepreneurship is the willingness to follow your dreams and feel certain about what others perceive as a risk." Your dream is your own and no one else's. And that's why when you decide to follow it, you will see it as a certainty while people around you might perceive it as a risk. All you will need to do is keep on following it until you achieve it. That is when you become an entrepreneur.

Going to a bookish perspective, coming from the French language and literally meaning "someone who undertakes", the dictionary meaning of the word 'entrepreneur' is "someone who engages in business enterprises, often with some personal financial risk."

The term 'entrepreneur' was made famous by the economist Jean Baptiste Say. In the early 1800s, he used the term to refer to individuals who create value in an economy by moving resources out of areas of low productivity, into areas of higher productivity and greater yield. In 1848, economist John Stuart Mill used the term in his very popular book, *Principles of Political Economy.* To Mill, the distinguishing feature of entrepreneurs was that they assume both the risk and the management of a business. The capitalist, on the other hand, may just put in the money without looking into the day-to-day business; while the manager would not worry about the finance but just run the business in an orderly manner.

Joseph Schumpeter in the 20th century emphasised that entrepreneurs are innovators who implement change in an economy by trying new combinations of resources. In the Schumpeterian view, the entrepreneur was a disruptive force in an economy. However, he emphasised that this process of creative destruction (the introduction of new things and the failing of old ones) was the critical ingredient necessary for economic progress. In contrast, Israel Kirzner viewed the entrepreneur as essentially an arbitrageur, who finds previously unnoticed profit opportunities and acts on them, moving the market towards a stable equilibrium. "Entrepreneurship does not consist of grasping a free ten-dollar bill which one has already discovered to be resting in one's hand; it consists in realising that it is in one's hand and that it is available for the grasping," wrote Kirzner in his book *Competition and Entrepreneurship* (Chicago: University of Chicago Press, 1973: p. 47.)

Debbie Fields, founder of the very famous and yummy *Mrs. Fields Cookies* said, "The important thing is not being afraid to take a chance. Remember, the greatest failure is to not try. Once you find something you love to do, be the best at doing it."

Entrepreneurship is just that. It's all about taking the chance, as well as the risk.

The most crucial element is to – Make the First Move. It's that elementary. Ideas are available everywhere. A lot of people have ideas, but there are not many who will execute it. It's not about having enough capital or the know-how. Money will come and go. Knowledge can be gained. But can the move be made? The answer to this question is not a 'NO'. It is a simple 'YES'. The move can always be made. But then, when has the move to be made? It can be made this week, next week or next month. It could also be made the next year or 3 years down the line. But that's not entrepreneurship. A real entrepreneur is not a delayer. A true entrepreneur is a doer.

An entrepreneur by heart always remains one. Richard Branson of the Virgin Enterprises says, "Business opportunities are like buses: there's always another one coming." That is very true. Businesses come and go. They become a hit. They die out. But the entrepreneur remains. The entrepreneur remains to start a new business, to venture again into uncharted waters and to realise a dream all over again.

He is a person who takes the risk of organising and operating a new business venture. He is not a manager or a capitalist. An entrepreneur has a dual job. He is both. As a capitalist, he pumps in the capital for the venture. As a manager, he looks after the business and creates a proper and well-balanced organisation.

Entrepreneurs are leaders who are the heart of a business. The essence of leadership means inspiring a group to come together for a common goal. Leaders motivate, console and work with people to keep them bonded and eager to move forward. That means setting a direction for the company, communicating it to everyone who will listen (and not everyone will listen) and keeping the morale high when times get tough.

Managers are the brains of the business. They establish the systems, create the required set of rules and aim to make the systems more efficient. A manager is someone who has been hired to look after the organisation of the company. He has had formal training in managing a company in order to achieve its aims and objectives. However, the entrepreneur has the responsibility to create those aims and objectives and motivate his managers to accomplish the goals.

Entrepreneurship requires the right mix of leadership skills and management skills. Leadership skills provide the direction, while management skills provide the systems that let a company grow successfully.

The profile of an entrepreneur is ever changing. More and more businesses are now being started by people who have not walked the earth for even three decades. The boardrooms are opening to people who are still in their twenties. The age for entrepreneurship is coming down. The entrepreneur is now being redefined into that person who is young and full of a burning desire to make it big and has the strength to go through the whole way. He is disciplined in his mind and creative in his heart to make his idea into reality.

He is emerging out to be a natural leader who has the ability to motivate his team to achieve higher efficiency and work in a more effective manner. Today, an entrepreneur is rising above all barriers and is developing an eye to see the world as one. He is to create a business which is not dependent on people only but is in fact, independent of them. Today, entrepreneurship requires creating a process-oriented business, where the entrepreneur can take a holiday from work at any time and the business will continue normally. An employee who seems crucial to the working of the company can quit, but the business will run smoothly because someone else will take his place. The entrepreneur is developing the knack to rise above the worldly barriers and see everything together. That makes his thinking clear, making it crucial to the success of the entrepreneur.

Entrepreneurship is that career which requires you to make the move at every step; with clear-cut thinking, unbound by the boundaries of the world and supported by sustained passion and fire. An entrepreneur is that person who will go ahead and make the move and then be ready to face what may come.

'Entrepreneurship' is a beautiful word, just like 'relationship', 'friendship', 'partnership' or 'companionship'. The four-letter word 'ship' is what makes it so special. In historic times, a voyage across seas and oceans was considered to be a very dangerous undertaking. It was common knowledge that once someone embarked on an ocean voyage, either the entire crew and passengers reached the distant shore or the ship capsized and sank or was set adrift after being raided by pirates who would swiftly execute all hands onboard. Fact and fiction are replete with heroes who survived hazards like storms at sea or pirates.

Entrepreneurship is very much like a dangerous sea crossing. Once you embark on the journey of entrepreneurship with fellow entrepreneurs, there is no way of stopping the ship and getting off. Either you will all reach your destination, or the ship will sink midway. But if the team sticks together and works its way tenaciously through storms, seasickness, dangerous rocks, whirlpools and cruel pirates, the destination is sure to be reached.

2

Essentials of Entrepreneurship

Is it about security? Security is the most important consideration in today's times. There are various forms of security that an individual desires, most crucial among them being job security in the profession and financial security, which is required throughout life.

The entrepreneur's life is full of risks, and 'security' is a word that's farthest away from him. But the ultimate aim is to be secure and in a safe zone. An entrepreneur always remains one by heart and seldom stops taking risks but, as time progresses, the entrepreneur aims at taking risks that are based on a level of security such that he can take even bigger ones.

Security and risks have a very integrated relationship. When one is insecure, the risk is difficult to take but taking the plunge and taking the risk may remove that insecurity once and for all. On the other hand, that plunge could even have the force to take the entrepreneur so deep down into the waters that coming afloat may never be possible again. When one is secure, the entrepreneur wants to take a bigger risk to take his potential to the limit. That is one characteristic of a great entrepreneur: his risk-taking ability – to achieve more and more in life – never ceases to exist.

Job security means to have a steady job with a steady income so that every morning one does not have to deal with the fear of being handed a firing slip. Now how could an entrepreneur NOT have job security? Yes, of course! He created the company. No one can kick him out. No one would dare to. But what about the company itself? He is the last one to cut a pay cheque for himself. He cannot do so till his venture stabilises. He has to make sure that his employees get their share on time. So there is no security till then. Further, a single bad move can wipe out the whole business; and while the employees will not sit in a sinking ship, the entrepreneur will have to sweat it out to prevent it from sinking. If it sinks, he cannot jump out of it but will have to go down with it. How long he can stay afloat depends on his grit. But the security is not there.

So entrepreneurship is not about getting job security: it is about creating it for himself and his employees.

So what is an entrepreneur made of?

It's the fire inside an entrepreneur which sets him apart from the rest of the world. The burning desire to create and follow a dream is what keeps the entrepreneur going. A clear, outcome-oriented mind with rock-solid determination is required to be an entrepreneur.

Knowledge

The brain of an entrepreneur is full of knowledge. The idea with which it all starts – from the dream surrounding the idea, to the plan surrounding the dream to make it a reality – are all there in the mind of the entrepreneur. He has not jumped into unknown waters without any research. A proper outcome-based approach rests in the mind of the entrepreneur who dreams of making it big. The mind must be powerful enough to control the heart, as tough decisions would need to be taken along the way. Knowledge is a strong tool and can make a lot of difference. Ideas are available everywhere and more often than not, more than a handful are trying to start the same idea. Even if the idea is totally unique, once it is implemented and is a little successful, someone will surely come up with the same plan all over again. So the mind plays a very important role. The more knowledge there is, the more clear the business plan and its implications in the mind become, and the easier it is to achieve the goal. The brain alone cannot do wonders, but without knowledge, there would be no start. Businesses without a proper approach are short-lived. A methodical approach is one of the most crucial ingredients in the recipe of a perfect business.

Vision

The brain provides not only the knowledge, but also the vision. The vision stems out of the knowledge itself. It opens up your mind to not what is at present, but what could be in the future. It gives you a path to follow. The path is a good motivator at times. The entrepreneur must make sure that the vision is crystal clear in his mind; else he will try his hand at places where he is not supposed to at that point of time. A clear vision will help to eliminate mistakes to a greater degree. No plan is perfect, but a brain with knowledge helps one come nearer to perfection.

Ego

The brain has another vital component – the ego. It is important, because an entrepreneur would face a lot of challenges in his journey and really needs the belief that he is right. It comes from the super-confidence that an entrepreneur has in himself and his idea, and not over-confidence. Over-confidence would be dangerous, but super-confidence is sheer strength of the mind.

Goal

The entrepreneur also has a mission statement in his mind for his entrepreneurial venture. This is possible only if he is absolutely clear on what he wants and desires.

Passion

Passion is what an entrepreneur has in his heart. Passion to go ahead and make the move. Passion to achieve the dreams and aspirations captured in his heart. Without passion, all the knowledge in the brain is a waste. If two or more people have the same idea, the one with the passion to go through with it will be a clear-cut winner. Passion comes out of love for one's work. An entrepreneur without passion is no entrepreneur at all. He is just a farce, trying his hand at something for which he is not cut out for. Passion gives rise to motivation. An entrepreneur differs from any other person because he does not work solely on motivation from the outside world, but rather from self-motivation which he derives from the passion that he carries for his venture. This self-motivation drives him day after day, night after night, to achieve more.

The life of an entrepreneur is a journey with no final destination for him as long as he has the passion for what he does. All the entrepreneurs whose names you may know today had very high levels of passion and self-motivation in their hearts. They are extremely passionate towards what they do, and they do it with full certainty and dedication. Passion is a desirable characteristic for everyone, but entrepreneurship is one career option which cannot do without it at all. While on this journey of entrepreneurship, many a time they find themselves alone and without any friends and supporters. At these times, it is difficult to get out of bed and start a new day. But passion ensures that one tides over all the troubles and continues the journey ahead. Passion is truly innate. Only if an entrepreneur has a strong passion for his work will he be able to continue it in a positive frame of mind and enjoy it. Else, work will feel like work and finally become a burden.

Fire

Fire is what brings both passion and knowledge together. Fire for that never-ending success is very important for an entrepreneur. The fire in his belly to go ahead with the idea about which he is passionate brings about the execution of the plan. The fire is needed to rise above all else and move forward with every step. Fire is required to fan the flame of passion even more. It is important to crush any competition which may come in your path. The passion gets one out of the bed to start the day, day after day, while the fire ensures that you complete the day with all the tasks which were to be done on that day. An entrepreneur should have such a fire in his belly that it can stimulate anyone with enthusiasm on the one hand, while on the other hand, it has the ability to burn anyone who stands in the way.

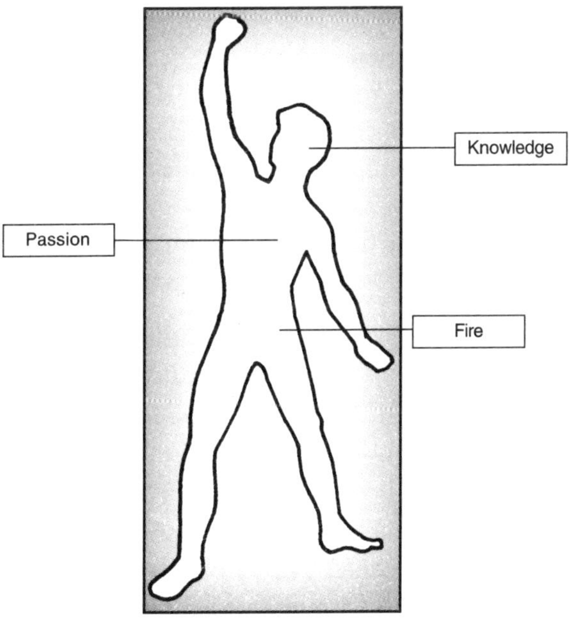

Anatomy of an Entrepreneur

A knowledgeable mind which has passion in the heart and fire in the gut is the anatomy of the entrepreneur. He is the one who continues on the journey of entrepreneurship and achieves success as desired and envisioned by him.

Before you plunge into the ocean of entrepreneurship, you need to ask yourself some questions. These questions, although very basic in nature, form the very core of entrepreneurship. The first and foremost one is:

Are you willing to work long hours and make the sacrifices necessary to get your business going?

This is crucial. The basic difference in a conventional job and entrepreneurship is that it will require much longer working hours. You will have to be the first one to reach the workplace and the last one to leave. You should instil this feeling in your whole team. The working days will be seven days a week for weeks, or maybe a few years to come. The hours may stretch up to 10-12 in a day. You will need to have enough stamina to cope with that kind of physical and emotional strain.

You will have to make sacrifices at a personal level. Along with that, there needs to be a delicate balance between family, friends and work. This is really important, because if there is imbalance in any one of them, then it will result in inefficiency at work. Support from the family is very important, as your loved ones' approval will do wonders for you, while their lack of interest may cause you to lose motivation.

Do you want to bear the responsibility for all business decisions and responsibilities related to your company?

The interesting aspect to this question is that any good decision that you will make, someone is going to come along and brag about it and take credit for it. However, if (God save you!) you make a bad decision, your team will remind you about it for years to come. They will do it sometimes just for the heck of it, while other times they'll be serious. You will have to be strong and accept all decisions made by you and your team.

Being an entrepreneur brings along with it a bag full of responsibilities. Your whole team will look up to you as a father-figure, even though you may be half their age. You will have to look after them, ensure that they get their bread and butter before you, and be a part of all their sorrows and joys. Notice that I say 'sorrows' before 'joys'. Sometimes along the way, you will find an employee in your team who will think you are young and incompetent. Now this person may prove to be a crucial resource for you at that point of time and it may be difficult for you to remove him from the team. Such times will require you to be a responsible entrepreneur with a mature head on your shoulders. It will be entirely up to you to develop projects, organise your time, and follow through on details.

Are you committed to entrepreneurship?

Commitment is very special in entrepreneurship. There will be times when you feel that it's just not worth it to put in so much of hard work and sacrifices and that life would be much better in a fixed job with fixed timings and a fixed salary. However, at times like these, your commitment will be tested. You might start receiving offers from various employers to join their organisation. You will need to understand that opportunities will always be there to attract you towards them. You will need to remain committed towards your passion of entrepreneurship. The saying "the grass is always greener on the other side" is quite true. However, entrepreneurship requires you to embed it in your belief system that your grass is not only the greenest but you also have the best bed of grass with you. Your commitment will be the strength of your belief system.

Are you ready to serve multi-roles within your organisation?

Initially, the organisation will be small and you might be the CEO, the CFO and the marketing manager all rolled into one. You might even be the cleaner and the receptionist of your organisation. You will have to be up to playing different roles in the organisation from time to time. Roles as different as day and night. All these roles, big and small, will teach you different aspects of the business. These roles will make you love your business even more than ever before and you will realise how each of these roles is important for the organisation. As time will progress, you will find your role getting clearer and more concise but it will be your experience of multiple roles in the initial stages that will teach you how to handle your team in a disciplined and more efficient manner.

Your organisation is your baby. There is no too small or too big a work for it. All are equally important. As the baby grows, your responsibilities will change and become different at different stages.

How well do you get along with different personalities?

Entrepreneurs need to develop working relationships with a variety of people including customers, vendors, staff, bankers, and professionals such as lawyers, accountants or consultants. You will need to deal with a demanding client, an unreliable vendor, or a cranky receptionist. You might not like someone, but he or she may be crucial for your business. At that point of time you will have to be able to deal with the person in a mature manner.

3

Initial Phase of Entrepreneurship

"I am an entrepreneur by any definition, but not in any heroic sense. I had no brilliant flashes of inspiration, no spectacular recognition of market need, no marvelous coincidence of being in the right place at the right time. I slugged it out in my chosen profession, making lots of errors and, fortunately, lots of good decisions."

—Joseph Jacobs, Chairman, Jacobs Engineering Group.

What Joseph Jacobs says is totally true for entrepreneurship. The initial phase is all about the focus. It is about slogging it out in your chosen field and working hard. You will make a lot of mistakes. And maybe a few good decisions here and there. The chairman of Jacobs Engineering Group made a number of good decisions. After all, it is one of the world's largest providers of technical services with more than 70 offices in a dozen countries and revenues of approx $5 billion! So making even a few good decisions will enable you to make a successful venture of your start-up!

So how does one go about the initial phase of this journey?

Sometimes, the idea to start something just may not strike. It's not a bad scenario. You can simply do what may be called an "I hate it when ...." list. This basically means that you write down what all you don't like about this world. This could be small or trivial, large or complex. You may not like the fact that when the water tap or shower is turned on in the cold winters, in the first couple of minutes cold water flows out and you have to wait for the hot water. Or you may not like that even if you polish your shoes for an appointment, very often when you reach there, they do not look perfect and you want to do something concrete about it. Or that there are no soft drinks available on the toll road and you have to make a diversion to actually get one.

Whenever you find yourself not liking something, write it down and when you have a certain number of issues on the list, write methods in which you may be able to solve them. See if there is an interesting idea in it. If a possibility exists, follow up on it. It may just lead you to the greatest invention possible! It may provide you with a start of the idea you were always waiting for. And that you would really like following it simply because it will help remove something which you do not like, and make your life simpler and more comfortable.

Another method of finding an idea to start a new venture is to go into yourself and find your hobbies. If your chosen profession can be from your hobbies, you will achieve a high level of satisfaction from it. If you like playing video games, you might want to start a venture which has play stations involved. If you love music, you might want to improvise with the musical instruments or want to create software for the easy creation of music. If you are a fitness freak, you might want to develop interesting fitness routines. The options are many. The trick is to choose one of them and just start or "make the move".

If you find something to do that you love doing and can convert into your profession, you will love your profession. You will enjoy your work and your efficiency will be at its highest. Because you will enjoy what you are doing, you will be in a lovey-dovey mood. After working hours, going home will be a pleasure because you would have had a good day and will enjoy the hours after office even more. Thus, the total day will turn into an enjoyable one, where you will look forward to going to work and working hard, and then going back to your friends and family and relaxing.

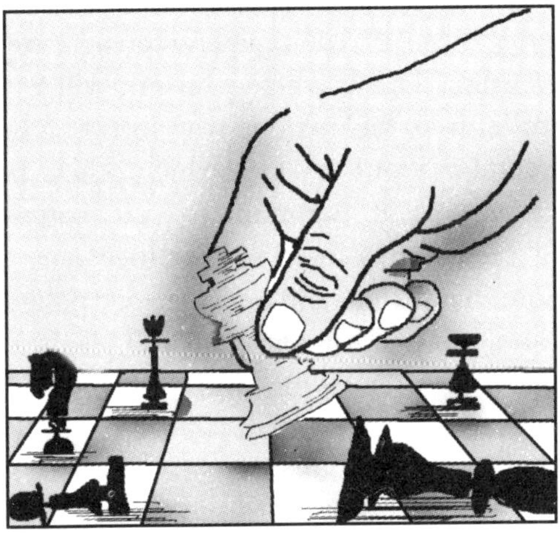

Motivators and Demotivators

So, entrepreneurship is all about following your dream with full commitment and passion until you achieve it. That is why one initiates it. Entrepreneurship has its rewards, which come after a lot of hard work. But then, is there any field where hard work is not required? Probably not. And more so in entrepreneurship. Here, the hard work needs to be embedded in a layer of confidence in yourself that what you are doing is correct and that you will go ahead in spite of all the road blocks and the demotivators you will bump into along the way. You will go ahead with or without the support of others if you truly want to do it. The lack of motivation will come from two different groups of people. One may be randomly associated, who would comment on your starting of a new venture and tell you about the risks involved in it. However, this group is more likely to be jealous of your risk-taking ability and will wonder what it would take to develop such a spirit in themselves. These people, not being close to you, should not affect you in any way.

The other group will be friends and family – people that are really close to you and who care for you. Their views will really matter to you because they always have in the past. Now this is a group where you will find that most of your loved ones are security-driven and perceive entrepreneurship as a highly risk-taking venture. This is where your grit will come into the picture. A real entrepreneur is one who feels one hundred and ten percent certain about the idea which others perceive as a risk. If their support is important to you, you will have to transfer your certainty to them so that they start believing in your idea more than before and become your pillar of strength. In case this does not happen, you must still go ahead with your venture. As things start falling into place, your loved ones would start seeing the happiness in you for your profession and in turn become positive about it.

Hard Times

Initially, there will be a lot of hard times. At times you will speculate as to why, in the first place, you chose to jump into the sea of entrepreneurship. You will wonder in what moment of madness you took that decision. You might want to shut down everything and just return to a job, something which might not be what you really want, but which would not entail the kind of stress and tension an entrepreneurial venture brings with it. Wrong decisions will form a part of the initial hard times. Sometimes the decision might be based on emotional responses more than commercial responses and they will lead to disastrous consequences. An interesting thing we noted while pursuing our entrepreneurial venture was that while decisions in the very initial times were taken very fast, as time passed, each decision took more and more time. In the early times, deciding to spend Rs. 45,000 on an advertisement in the newspaper was easier than making a decision of spending Rs. 20,000 on a campaign now. It's not because we have become slow. It's because we have become mature and now know that each and every decision matters and must be taken only after full scrutiny.

Paying Yourself

You will be the entrepreneur, the visionary and the dreamer. Along with all this, you will also be the salary provider. You will have to pay your employees on time, always. It is you who will get paid right at the last. We took our first salary after thirteen months of operations. In this lies a catch. By not paying a salary to yourself, you may feel that you are sacrificing so much for your dream venture. However, in reality, it may start affecting your self-esteem as the chances are that all the people around you will be earning money in their jobs. It is very important for you to realise that not taking your salary, although is an act of great sacrifice, will not be good for your motivation. Drawing a salary out of your own venture is a validation of your hard work. It is proof to yourself that you are working towards a bigger goal. So you will have to make a conscious effort to earn enough, not only to give salaries to your employees on time, but also to yourself.

Multiple-role Dilemma

You will also face a multiple-role dilemma in the initial days. You will need to understand that in a small start-up, you will be taking the roles of the Director, the Finance Officer, the Marketing Manager and even the Cleaner all in the same day. This might lead to a confused feeling inside you and bog you down. But then, it will be these multi-role tasks which will develop in you qualities which you will utilise in your business throughout. These tasks will explain to you the importance of the processes which you will ultimately develop for your business. We still remember the Sunday in the early days, when there were just two of us in the office, sitting and completing our work when one of our important clients called and said that he was in Delhi and would like to drop by our office if we were around. Within the next 15 minutes, we had cleaned the office, set up the chairs properly, kept glasses of water on the table and made an agenda for the meeting. He entered on the stroke of the twentieth minute.

But in those twenty minutes, we had played the roles of the cleaner, office administrator, manager and the director!

Legal Aspects

On the legal side, you could either start a company or enter into a partnership.

1. A Partnership Firm is a sum total of persons who have come together to share the profits of the business carried on by them or any of them. It does not have a separate legal entity. A Company is an association of persons who have come together for a specific purpose. The Company has a separate legal entity as soon as it is incorporated under law.
2. Liability of the partners in a Partnership is unlimited. However, the liability of shareholders of a Limited Company is limited to the extent of unpaid share or to the tune of the unpaid amount guaranteed by the shareholder.
3. Property of the Firm belongs to the partners and they are collectively entitled to it. In case of a Company, the property belongs to the Company and not to its members.
4. A partner cannot transfer his shares in a Partnership Firm without the consent of all other partners. In case of a Company, shares may be transferred without the

permission of the other members, in the absence of any provision to the contrary in the Articles of Association of the Company.

5. In case of a Partnership, the number of members must not exceed 20 in case of banking businesses and 10 in other businesses. A Public Company may have as many members as it desires subject to a minimum of 7 members. A Private Company cannot have more than 50 members.
6. There must be at least 2 members in order to form a Partnership Firm. The minimum number of members necessary for a Public Limited Company is 7 and 2 for a Private Limited Company.
7. In case of a Partnership, 100% consensus is required for any decision. In case of a Company, decision of the majority prevails.
8. On the death of any partner, the Partnership is dissolved unless there is provision to the contrary. On the death of the shareholder, the Company's existence does not get terminated.

After you decide whether you want to start your venture as a partnership or a company, the next important step will be to open a bank account. This will require you to produce certain documents depending upon the kind of entity you want to form, i.e., partnership or a company.

Once these two steps are over, you will be ready to start your business! More steps such as applying for a service tax or a value added tax number will come on the way. To keep you on the correct side of the law, it will be advisable to hire a chartered accountant to take care of these steps, else these would consume a fairly large chunk of your mindshare and timeshare, that you could better employ by concentrating on your venture.

4

Understanding Finance

Money is both an ingredient for a business and the final desired outcome of a business. So entrepreneurship is a lot about money. An entrepreneur must know from where to get his funds to start the business as well as how to manage them.

As an ingredient, money is the single most important factor why a lot of people with wonderful ideas, and the zeal to implement them never got started. They might not have had any capital to start, or could not find any investors for their plans. However, that should not stop you from taking a plunge into the world of entrepreneurship. Take a loan or borrow from someone and start what you want to start.

Many of the top businesses of today had their founders sleeping on the roads or in oil mills or having to start their businesses in their garages. Many of those got wiped out in their first month or even in the first five years. But the ones which had passionate people behind them, flourished. They flourished not with or without capital but with their personal satisfaction and a never-ending desire. It may take time to break even and even more time to start drawing a salary, but then entrepreneurship is a game, just like Monopoly. The more risk one takes, the more chances are there to rise. In a game of Monopoly, we are happy to "risk" paying for a few houses, to raise the rent when someone lands on our property. But in real life, when it comes to taking a risk with 'real' houses or 'real' business activities, our risk-taking abilities suddenly take a back seat. That's because it's not 'play money' any more. This is our own hard earned money we are talking about. This is what gives us food and shelter.

An entrepreneur sees his business as a game, and money is just a way to keep score. This is the difference between the employee and entrepreneurial way of thinking.

Money will start coming in slowly and from a company of just its founder(s), it will grow bigger and will have employees. Then will start a new dilemma. The employees will have to be paid. So you start working harder. You earn the money and then at the end of the month, give it as salary to the employees!

Managing Money

You have to keep tabs on the bank statement every second so you know that the next cheque to be written would not bounce. There would be days when you would want to splurge a little extra on the company as there is some money in the account; and days you would find yourself transferring money from your personal account into the company account because you fear a cheque bouncing.

Capital Resources (Debt funding, Equity funding)

The capital resources may be low. So what? Be creative, resourceful and make realistic plans to manage the finances. Remember, you are still playing Monopoly.

There are various ways to raise money for your start-up. Most of the funding falls under one of two categories.

Debt funding is when you take a loan which has to be paid back together with the interest accumulated over a period of time. This will generally have fixed obligations to pay amounts of money according to a schedule.

On the other hand, there is equity funding. This is when the fund provider (investor) receives a percentage ownership (shares) in your company that grows proportionally to the overall value of your company. In the event of the sale of the company or an Initial Public Offering (IPO) to the stock markets, the investors who are also equity holders, can cash out their stock, ideally receiving a large return for taking the risk early on. Here, an investor will also get dividends according to his ownership percentage but generally has no obligation to return on any capital.

Loans

There are various types of loans which you can take. They include personal loans from friends or family members or loans from a bank. In case you take loans from people known to you, you might even convert these loans into stock options for them later on. The provision of debt capital has the 'pro' of reduction in risk of financing. In case of bankruptcy, the loan has to be paid back before the distribution of any assets to the stockholders. However, the 'con' here is that debt financing generally does not have any interest of the investor in the company and thus does not contribute to the growth of the company.

If you go for equity financing, you will generally approach venture capitalists or angel investors. Venture capital is capital provided by outside investors for financing of new, growing or struggling businesses. Venture capital investments are generally high risk investments but offer the potential for above average returns. A venture capitalist (VC) is a person who makes such investments. A venture capital fund is a pooled investment vehicle (often a partnership) that primarily invests the financial capital of third-party investors in enterprises that are too risky for bank loans. An angel investor is someone who invests in a business venture, providing the capital for start-up or expansion. Often these individuals are looking for a higher rate of return than would be given by more traditional investments, and will be looking to play an active role in the management of the company. In exchange for the investment, the investor can benefit from the growth of the company and receive either common or preferred stock. Here, the 'pros' are that the VC or the angel investor will actively participate in the functioning of your company and you will benefit from his vast experience. He will actually contribute to the growth of the company. However, generally, when a VC comes into the picture, you tend to lose control over the company as now he is also a crucial shareholder of your company and will be interfering to a large extent.

How to get Funds?

Obtaining funding is exactly like going for an interview for a job. You need to be thoroughly prepared! Here are some tips which you can use.

1. If you do not want a large amount for your business plan, then you might first want to try and approach your family or close friends. You can fix up a certain rate of interest with them and take money from them as a personal loan.
2. If you have any assets such as a house or a car in your name or a sizeable balance in your bank account, you can approach a bank for a loan. You will have to assure the bank that there is really no risk in giving you a loan. Remember that a bank always wants to lend money (that's their job!), but they want to lend it only after feeling 100% secure.
3. Now, in case your business requires higher amounts of funds to get it started, you will need to be a lot

more serious on how to raise the money with maximum efficiency. It is here that the importance of the business plan asserts itself. Your business plan should be complete and professionally sound and stable when you approach any VC or angel investor for a large funding. Your plan will need to be self-explanatory – who you and your team members are, what is the basic concept of the product or service you are offering, the market research, the target segment, amount of money needed, how and where will the money be spent, the expected revenue generation and the profit. One thing that shows you are serious is if you form a private limited company and then approach for funding. The reason is that in such a way, you are able to express to the investor that you have already taken some concrete steps towards starting your business. Most VC firms receive thousands of business plans per year and can only give five to ten minutes per plan to decide if there is really any strength in it or not. So if you know someone who is inside one of these firms, get your business plan hand delivered to the people who matter.

4. If you are still a minor, get an adult involved with you whom you trust totally. You will have to behave a little older than what you actually are! One good trick is to learn the financial lingo! If you can talk in the banker's language, nothing like it. If you show that you have a grasp of accounting and general business knowledge, you may very well be able to obtain the loan or financing you need.
5. Another thing that helps to get equity financing is if you have a strong board of advisors backing you up. This will help the angel investor to develop more trust in your venture.

6. Talk to people who might have taken loans or funding recently. Ask them what formalities bankers or investors usually ask for. Take references of good investors from them. It is better to be more prepared when you go to someone to ask for money. He might not give you a second chance to talk to him.

Before we proceed to the financial management part of your business, we should remember that there are some fatal mistakes which you might end up making. Avoid taking any decisions relating such areas as long as possible. In case you have to make them, then be thoroughly prepared for the results.

1. Enough capital not raised at the first instance:

   Remember that you cannot apply to the same company over and over again for getting the same job done, if you have not succeeded at the very first go itself. Similarly, it is very difficult to go back to your banker or investor for more money soon after you get started. He will take it as a danger sign that something is surely going wrong or that you have no idea of what you are into. This situation generally comes when the business plan that you made was too optimistic. Spend the maximum time in determining how much funds you need to start and sustain the business. Also, while calculating the revenue generation and profits, adopt a more pessimistic approach for the business plan. That does not mean that you do not aim higher, it just means that you are better prepared with the finances.

2. Putting at risk everything that you own:

   There might be salary days when you might not be able to pay yourself. Depending upon the gestation period of your business, ensure that you keep a reserve for yourself which will provide you the money to continue your life without any hassles.

3. Potential risks in borrowing from friends and family:

   Although debt financing can be done by borrowing from your closest friends or the family, ensure that you have all the terms clearly written down in black and white, and fully agreed upon. You must make certain that they know of all the risks involved in your venture. You must disclose all the information that might be critical to the business. Remember to keep the professional and the personal relationships with the same person as separate as possible.

4. Improper keep of financial records:

   Your investors and the banker will want proper financial records from time to time. When you start your own business, you will want to earn more and more and feel that the records can be sorted out later. However, it becomes too late and the presence of outdated records comes to haunt you when the financial year nears closing. At such a time, making of proper records will eat up too much of your productive time. It will also cause a lot of trouble and embarrassment for you in front of your investors. So you must ensure that you have your excel sheets and the accounting software running from Day One itself.

Finance Management

Getting money for your business is just one of the parts of finance. Now that you have your company up and running, you really need to ensure you grow it, rather than lose.

We had many a sleepless night thinking what if a cheque bounced in the morning, and we found hired goons outside our houses demanding cash in exchange of the bounced cheque or the police sending an arrest warrant for a fraudulent transaction. Once it happened that one of us actually woke up at 4:00 a.m. and logged on to the Net, into his personal bank account, and transferred money into the company's account because the calculations in his sleep suggested that a particular cheque would bounce the next morning! This is the kind of situation we do not want to be in! Sleep is definitely more precious than getting up in the middle of the night and logging on to transfer money.

There are two kinds of financial days in an entrepreneurial venture:

1. Bad Days – when the money from the bank account just seems to be going out and out. These are the days when there are too many cheques to be issued and you, being the Financial Officer, will wish that the cheque leaves get exhausted!
2. Good Days – when there is money in the account and it seems that the money is not going anywhere. A funny kind of positive, confident feeling will come over you, that you are the owner of all this money.

However, in the start-up stage, there is a tendency to overspend. And the saying that good days are always followed by bad days and vice versa is quite true! It happens that after a good day, you suddenly get the urge to buy a fax machine because you feel your office should definitely have one (though the number of faxes that you are sending or receiving are less than even 20 per month!). So you go and buy one and issue the cheque. The next few days see less business, or no revenue generation...and the bad days are back!

It is important not to curb the expenditure too much, as that might start hampering the creativity of the minds of the people behind the business. However, you must ensure that money is not being spent according to anyone's whims or fancies.

There are certain important steps which you need to take so as to consolidate your business financially:

1. Formation of at least two bank accounts

You must create at least two bank accounts from the first day of your business. One of the accounts will serve as the incoming revenue account, while the second one will serve as the expense account. This will help you better control your finances from the starting. The thumb rule is that you can never directly issue an expense cheque from the revenue account. The money must first be transferred into the expense account before it can be spent. This curbs impulsive spending to a large extent.

You might even want to create more bank accounts where one could be a tax payment account (money deposited to be paid as taxes at the end of the financial year), different revenue accounts for different revenue streams (so that you can easily calculate what part of the business is profitable, when and why it is so), etc. We will not deny that the paperwork will increase considerably with each bank account opened. However, with online banking now being very active, multiple accounts can be managed far more easily than ever before. It will take some time to get into the groove of it, but once you become habituated to it, the amount of peace that will prevail in your professional lives will be worth the initial effort. Moreover, investors and bankers will also get a very clear picture of the finances of the company by referring to statements of the various accounts.

2. Asset creation

"There is only one way to make a great deal of money, and that is in a business of your own."

– *J. Paul Getty, former oil tycoon and once the richest man in America.*

This is the basis of any business or commercial venture – to make money. As an entrepreneur and owner of your own business, it is your responsibility that the money coming into the company is not all going out and actually adding up to the personal wealth of the owners and to the assets of the company. One of the safest ways to create assets is to open fixed deposit accounts in your bank. A Fixed Deposit is like loaning the bank your money. In return, they pay you interest. There are various types of fixed deposits that you can open:

1. Profit Fixed Deposit – at least 10% of every month's revenue should go in the profit fixed deposit of that month. This will add to the company's assets.
2. Stakeholders' Fixed Deposit – at least 7% of every month's revenue should go into the stakeholders' deposit. This is your asset creation, which can be distributed among the stakeholders at the end of the financial year.
3. Salary Fixed Deposit – fixed deposits equal in value to the salaries of the owners can be opened. Here, the salary can be given to the business owners once in every four months.
4. Taxes Fixed Deposit – every month, you may put money into a fixed deposit which contributes to paying the taxes due at the end of the year.

There is no provision in any bank to put fixed deposits into these above heads. This division is for your internal financial management. What is happening is that the moment the money comes into the revenue account, it must be transferred into the various accounts that you have made. There the money is put into fixed deposits and blocked from direct usage. This way, you would have been able to create wealth for yourself and the company. The two most important fixed deposits are the ones relating to the stakeholders, and the profits. You will have to internally decide how much you want to put in each month into the fixed deposits depending upon the actual revenue generation of that month. However, you must aim to achieve your targets you had mentioned in the financial planning sheet of that month.

Now the question arises, if all the money coming in is going into the fixed deposits, where will the working capital come from? The 'Overdraft Account' (OD) comes into the picture here. The formal definition of an overdraft account is, "When the amount of money withdrawn from a bank account is greater than the amount actually available in the account, the excess is known as an 'overdraft' and the account is said to be 'overdrawn'. If agreed in advance by the bank, this is essentially a form of loan facility; if not agreed in advance by the bank, either penal charges may be incurred or the bank may bounce the cheques." So when you put money into the bank in the form of fixed deposits, you will arrange with the banker to give you overdraft facilities against the security of your fixed deposits. The rate of interest for this might be slightly higher than the rate attracted by your fixed deposit. However, this is offset by the fact that you are still earning interest for your fixed deposit and paying just slightly over it for a short period to the bank for temporarily using its wealth. This system helps you to create assets for the company.

The advantages are clearly visible:

1. You are creating wealth for the company which you can use anytime by availing the Overdraft facility.

2. The more the personal and company wealth creation, the more confident you will feel about your business.
3. You can go out to search for more funding from VCs or angel investors. They will really like the fact that you generated assets from your business.
4. You will work harder to ensure that the OD facility is not being used very frequently, because you have to pay a higher rate of interest to the bank.

Fixed deposits are one of the safest ways of asset generation. There are other ways available, like investing in the stock market, mutual funds and allied investments. However, these require more of your time. The returns are higher in these investments, but they are also vulnerable to the ups and downs of the financial markets. Thus the risk factor is also higher. In the initial stages of your business, you will not have enough time to devote to these investment methods. Thus, fixed deposits are really suited for asset creation for start-ups.

3. Cash flows

There is nothing more important than cash flow in the business. In fact, it is the lifeline of a business. Cash is absolutely critical for the growth and well-being of a business. "Cash" refers to those liquid assets that have immediate cash redemption value such as cash and cheques. Cash flow is defined as the cash money flowing in and out of the business. It is not the same as profitability. Cash inflow is the cash flowing into the business from all sources over a period of time. Cash outflow is the cash flowing out of the business from all sources over a period of time.

First-generation entrepreneurs must do proper planning and preparation for events that might occur in the future and affect the business, as well as the market changes which may totally change the direction of their business. The most important aspect of planning in the company is an effective cash flow management. One of the major reasons for a business to shut down is the failure in doing correct and proper cash flow management. Cash flow is important for various outcomes. It is used:

1. to manage the daily activities of the company such as paying various bills, rents, salaries of the employees, etc.
2. as a backup for unanticipated problems.
3. for potential investment purposes which may bring in good returns.

An Operating Cycle is defined as "the system through which cash flows from the purchase of inventory through the collection of accounts received." It measures the flow of assets into cash and is, in effect, a business stopwatch.

For example, in a product industry, you may deliver your product on the 15th of a month to your client and send your invoice to them. However, your client will be able to issue a cheque only on the 7th of next month when all their cheques are given out. Now you might have to pay for various pending bills of your own, which you would do through the money you received for your last month's executed orders. Through the orders you have sent on the 15th, you will only be able to pay next month's bills.

A cash flow analysis will show whether your daily operations generate enough cash to meet your business obligations. It also indicates how major cash outflows relate to major cash inflows. It will tell you if the inflows and outflows result in a positive cash flow from operations or in a net drain of funds. Cash flow analysis will help in identifying if there are any cash related problems. This will help to facilitate better control of cash flows and give enough time to plan and prepare for the growth of your business.

Regular meetings to discuss cash flow will have to be held, probably on a monthly basis. In the initial stages, the frequency can even be higher, even once a week. The development of a cash reserve account will enable you to plan expenditures for the following month. A monthly cash flow projection will help you to look at available funds and compare actual figures to past months. In case the figures which you projected are not being met up with, the financial plans must be altered to provide more cash. In case there is an excess of positive cash flow, it might mean that there has been more borrowing. Borrowed funds are costly, so they should be repaid at the earliest possible opportunity. Such money could be converted to fixed deposits or invested in better ways. The objective is to develop a plan that will provide a well-balanced cash flow.

Achieving a positive cash flow is critical for your venture. This will require a sound strategy. Some basic tips are:

1. You must ensure that you are collecting money for your services and products from your clients at the earliest.
2. In case there is a delay in receiving the payment, you will be required to tighten the credit requirements.
3. You will have to look at the pricing once again. You may be able to raise the price of your product or your service and still have the same customer base.
4. Increasing your customer base and trying out new promotional strategies will help you achieve higher revenue generation and thus better cash flows. However, you must be careful because many times a large portion of your sales would have been purchased on credit. When credit sales increase, accounts receivable also increase, not cash. Collection terms of receivables are usually 30 days after the purchase date, and sales expenses are most often incurred before receivables are collected.
5. You must use technology to analyse your cash flows. It's best to use financial management software where you can keep proper records.

Always remember that if you are able to keep your cash flows positive, you will flow really well in the business!

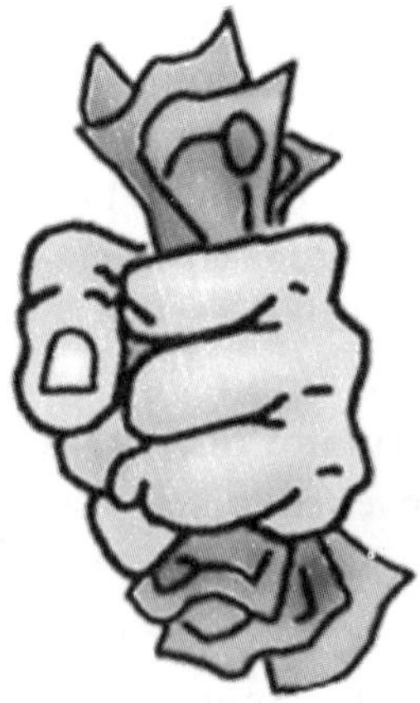

4. Tightening the grip on expenses

This is an important point to maintain healthy finances. Whenever you receive a payment from a client, a voice will be heard inside you that will tell you to go and spend that money in ten different areas which will supposedly help the company. However, at such times, you will have to tell yourself that all the money that comes in must not go out. It must actually contribute to the positive cash flow. Going back to the start of this chapter, buying a fax machine may add to the glamour of your office, but it may not really be serving any purpose at that point of time. So you will have to be strong and tell your inner voice that right now, such an expense is unwarranted and can be done later when cash flows are much stronger. Sometimes, tightening the expenses might start curbing the efficiency of the business. Such expenses should not be tightened, e.g., if your phone bills are higher than you expected they'd be. But the phone is a crucial element to your business; do not cut down on that aspect. It may just hamper your business. However, curbing on useless expenditures is important. You must instil in your employees and yourself a feeling of saving wherever possible, like using one-side-used paper for rough printouts, switching off extra lights at your workplace, ensuring that your local courier or the photostat vendor is not overcharging you. A little negotiation with the people you deal with will never hurt you, but will work in your favour. Keeping a check on these activities will help you bring down expenses by a considerable amount.

5. Cash now is better than cash later

This is one of the most universally accepted mantras in the world. While dealing with your customers, if you can make them pay you early by offering any incentive at that point of time, go ahead and do it. The advantages are obvious. It will help in positive cash flows. It will also help you reduce your (costly) bank overdraft. However, you will have to be careful in deciding what incentive you want to give to your client. Generally, it's an instant discount which you may offer ranging from 5-15%. This can become dangerous sometimes, as your reputation may become of one of those who earn the extra percentage over the normal norms of profit. Thus you might be forced to give this discount to all your clients irrespective of whether they are paying instantly or later. Other incentives can be to offer a discount voucher for the next interaction that your client will have with you. This will also help you cross-sell better. Another incentive for getting instant payments could be to give something free with your existing product or service which the customer can get only if he pays instantly. You will have to cultivate the habit of getting your payments made as soon as possible, else you risk getting a reputation among your clients of an extremely laid-back businessman who can be denied his payments for a longer duration.

6. Taxation

Taxation is a necessary evil. There might be different types of taxes in different countries. However, some of the common ones include Income Tax, Value Added Tax, Service Tax, Sales

Tax, etc. Although you might not like paying taxes, but there is nothing much you can do about it! You must have an informed Chartered Accountant working for you who can handle all issues related to taxation for you. Although having basic knowledge on taxation is not bad, do not try and spend too much time on it, as the laws can sometimes be very complicated, confusing and hard to understand. Until and unless you have done economics or accounting in your studies, most of the tax-related language will go over your head. Here, the rule of outsourcing comes into play, which means that you outsource your weakness to a professional who will take care of the issue on your behalf.

However, you must show a certain level of interest also in its working, as no one will know your business better than you and thus you and your accountant might be able to develop strategies through which your taxation may be reduced. As the financial planner of your company, you must put away a certain portion of your revenues every month towards the paying of taxes. This money might be put in a fixed deposit or just kept in the bank account. But it is necessary to keep this component separate every month, else the financial burden will pile up at the end of every financial year and disrupt all cash flows. Consider the money kept towards taxation as an expense to the company and this will contribute to the negative cash flow every month. However, the peace of mind you will achieve by keeping this component separate will be amazing. This will also motivate you to work harder so that you get your cash flows to be more and more positive!

5

Conversion to Serious Business

You will notice a change in writing style for this chapter. The reason is that this will vary from business to business and team to team. We are explaining this using the example of our baby – Appin.

We had done enough promotions till now. Our names had appeared in newspapers and the company started becoming known among the students. It was a big step for students to start a Private Limited. Company. However, we did not understand business well. We had taken the first step but were still not working as a serious business. There was no structure, no integration, no direction and no focus. We were still in the process of evolving the concept and learning many things but at the same time, we were pulling in different directions that would lead us nowhere. We started feeling that people were not looking at us as student entrepreneurs any longer. They had started seeing Appin as a company. Our energies were like the rays of the sun scattered in different directions. We needed a lens to focus and channelise our energy.

We started facing problems of loss of confidence and focus, financial setbacks and no business. Many times we put money from our own pockets into the business and forgot about it. We didn't maintain too many records of accounting transactions. We used to focus on what we would now call unimportant things. We were not even sure what we'd be doing the next day. We didn't have a full-time working team. Our business was running as a hobby business; not a serious one. We were committed but we needed a direction.

Then we realised that we had to change our focus; more into the business and less in promotions and just networking with people. This was the time when Anuj came to India for a while. He used to travel back and forth from USA. He taught us the basics of business, cash flows and other essentials that we weren't aware of. With this knowledge and focussing of energy, we started with more training programs and developed the concept of HomTech Certification courses which was a vision for the training industry in the future. With Anuj's help, we hired people who later went on to become real assets for the company. We then created a research laboratory to execute niche technology programs. These programs were extremely specialised and people started associating Appin with niche technologies. In the meantime, Anuj developed a team in USA and we created the first version of the HomTech products. The vision of HomTech was to replicate classroom teaching on your computer. We produced the first version of these courses prepared by top professionals and professors the world over. The product was 5% of what we envisioned of HomTech, but we were on the path. We understood that it would only be a matter of time before our HomTech courses revolutionised learning.

Appin started growing, and many corporations started inviting Appin technology evangelists for training their employees. The unique combination of people in Appin which included well-known professionals of the technical world, an active young force and experienced brains of alumni, guided the company well and we started growing at a very fast pace. Turning from a young start-up into a serious business was not an easy task. We faced our share of problems. With growth, we realised we had to become more disciplined in our way of working. It was opposed by the team in the beginning and took a while to be accepted in principle. The alignment andre-alignment of our beliefs took place very often. We faced a lot of operational problems as well. Our chairman Mr. Chandrashekhar along with Vipin, were instrumental in creating a successful operations process. It was a challenge to bring our team on that path, especially with the occasional hurdle or two. Sometimes it felt like we were going one step forward and two steps backward. But once the process set in, the ride was smoother and more hassle-free.

The Different Stages of Learning

There were different stages of learning that we passed through. Earlier, we were not in the habit of planning. We realised that for better results, planning is a necessity. The famous quote "Failing to plan is planning to fail" explains the importance of planning. This helped us in creating more realistic goals, and paths to be followed to achieve those goals. It was not easy to plan. Many a time, we did escape planning. When you don't plan, however, you don't spend your time in an effective way, thereby hurting the company badly. We instilled the habit of planning in the entire company. You will meet with resistance the first few times. Therefore, you must have effective and clear communication with your employees. First understand the importance of planning, and then pass that on in your work environment.

The next stage came when we started checking whether an activity was yielding the anticipated results or not. We realised that planning activities alone were insufficient. We had to implement those plans. Many times, you may plan but don't implement what you plan. Discussing the effectiveness of your plan is extremely important. And in the initial excitement, we even set a process. The first few days it might seem to work great. However, the key lies in being able to continue with that process each day, while strengthening it all the while. At this stage, we started producing some results and our quality of service and products improved considerably.

The third stage of learning was when our company, along with planning and checking the activities, started creating back-up plans. Whenever a plan was tried and failed, we had a back-up plan ready for action. In order to reach this stage, we went through our share of problems. However, if you are on the path of learning, your company will reach this stage soon.

Another development came when we started drawing our own salaries from the company. We never paid ourselves in the earlier months and re-invested whatever we earned, sometimes even investing money from our pockets. Now the situation changed completely. Along with drawing our salaries, we also started creating company assets like fixed deposits.

We realised that the process of transforming from a student business to a serious business was a 360° shift in one's psychology. In order to achieve this transformation, we faced many setbacks and broke many of our own blocks. Running a business is a very serious affair. You need to keep your team happy, take care of their salaries, provide quality to your customers and stay in the process of increasing the quality of all processes. Entrepreneurship is thus a very serious affair, as the lives of many depend on it. In fact, you must move into the psychology of a serious business from Day One, even if you are a student. You will start functioning as a company only when you understand these things.

A very important point while running a business is that you should pay yourself. We didn't take salaries in the initial stages thinking our business to be our baby. And surely, parents don't charge their babies! But business is different. Though your commitment may not be dependent on whether you receive salaries or not, it definitely gives you a reason to go that extra mile. Besides, you deserve that appreciation...and money is the fastest way of getting it.

6

Scaling the Business – "Realising the Vision"

There is a myth about scaling a business – that you must increase your products to scale your business. Scaling doesn't necessarily mean increasing the number of products you have. It means capturing a bigger market share of consumers and being able to reach out to more people.

For example, Microsoft began scaling its business by increasing sales channels in different countries, having different vendors and heavy-duty advertising. The prime product of Microsoft is an Operating System. They have established their brand as leaders in an operating system more commonly known as Windows. Today, Microsoft has sales channels, vendors and training vendors all over the world. They have captured around 80% of the world PC market. This is scaling in its truest sense.

Another example may be scaling an Internet business by increasing the site traffic using SEO (search engine optimisation), uploading more web pages, having more resellers and referrers, advertising at various places for different customers and buying out businesses similar to yours but more famous in a local territory. Perfect examples are of eBay buying baazee.com, a famous Indian online portal, or perhaps NIIT buying egurucool.com.

There are many businesses that always remain the way they had begun. There is a very common saying in the world of entrepreneurship, "Either the business will grow or the business will die." You will realise at some point of time that now is the time to scale the business and capture the market. You will know then that if you don't take this step soon, someone else will.

To understand the importance of when to scale is judged by another good statement which says, "The real entrepreneur is the person who understands that the success of a business lies in being at the right place at the right time." The timing and speed are both very important. In fact, Bill Gates in his book *Business @ the Speed of Thought* wrote that a business runs at the speed of its team. The team must be able to take business decisions fast.

We realised that our business now required moving to the next step, i.e., scaling the business to various countries. We were finding various ways such as Venture Capital. We tried two-three approaches which were not that successful, until we found what we had to do. Appin's expertise was in niche technical courses, very well-packaged and given by international trainers along with branding and market expertise. As Appin had people from all the communities – Academia, Industry and Students – it knew the training industry in depth. We realised that it was time to invite other established local players and transfer our expertise to them while maintaining the quality standards of Appin. Yes, the idea was similar to franchising. And the biggest challenge was maintaining the high quality standards.

Challenges

You will face challenges while going for this expansion plan (scaling the business). The primary ones are these questions:

1. What is your USP (Unique Selling Proposition)?
2. Why YOUR COMPANY?
3. How will you support your channel partners?
4. How will you make it operationally possible for channel partners all over the world?
5. How would you convince the first channel partner?
6. How would you protect your interests with theirs?
7. How would you keep them dependent on you?

All these questions are valid and need to be answered. And when you will find answers to these and implement them, your whole business model will be in front of your eyes. The global billion dollar business which you dreamt of will start becoming possible. These questions are very important for you to answer. For example, our USP was high-end technical expertise. Our strength was the brand, the Win-Win offering and so on.

It will take you some time to answer these questions. In fact, it might just be your customers and business associates who will help you in realising these answers.

The first major challenge is finding the right channel partner. It is ultimately the motivation and operational excellence of your channel partners that contributes to your quality as perceived by the customer. Thus, it is very important to find channel partners with a similar business interest and motivation. Be cautious here, as this could lead to problems later on. Another important requirement is maintaining a solid legal structure with the partners. Your legal agreements with the partners should be as per your goals and visions.

Another major challenge which businesses face in scaling is operational excellence. In fact, when a small company scales its business, it has to plan and re-plan for operational superiority. You need to invest more money into management and quality assurance. It involves benchmarking processes and quality checks. This is very important, because you have to immediately increase the production, manpower and many other expenses all at once. This leads to huge management problems. It's generally true that entrepreneurs enjoy this challenge. They always believe in solving management problems during this time in their business.

It is essential to give importance to your product or service at this time. You need to protect your product/service and idea while expanding your business. When Appin started scaling one of its businesses which dealt with selling computer-based programs, we faced threats of piracy and copying. The first step we took was getting trademarks, copyrights and patents on all our products. This would prevent someone from copying our brand name and intellectual property directly. We also secured our CDs so that no one could copy our content. Essentially, you have to protect the product/formula/service USP of the company before scaling, otherwise someone may copy it and begin a parallel business.

Another challenge is the transfer of the philosophy of the company while scaling the business. This is important for keeping the company's values and vision intact.

New problems come when you scale your business and hence you need to be prepared with a very strong support team. You must offer support services to your channel partners. This will not only help their business but will also build their trust and dependency on your company. The more you support your channel partners, the more benefits they yield for your business.

Quality : Constant and Never-ending Improvement is a Must

There should always be a continuous process of quality improvement for your product in the areas of marketing, sales, finance, customer support and human resource management. This is very important for the company to grow and prosper. This also gives confidence to the channel partners that the company supporting them is one of the leaders in the business, and is giving them superior products and services. One of the most important parts of scaling a business in today's world is the automation of processes. All the processes are generally supported by computers and this helps in increasing the speed of business as well as data maintenance. In the cyber age, there is rarely any big company that survives without strong technology integration with its processes. This is very important for the business.

Scaling a business helps you to understand the business in reality. You understand the market dynamics because you now play with volumes. You also understand the importance of processes and quality checks. Thus, in the real sense, the idea becomes a business when you scale it. The concept of the business now emerges, and matures. Your brand starts to evolve, bring up the question as to how you want your brand to be? As mentioned in the previous chapters, your brand can only be in one extreme. For example, Mercedes is only known for high-class cars. It is not known for cheap-segment cars. This is very important to understand. Especially before scaling your business, there is a possibility that you might have to kill some of your products. But it is very important that you scale a more focussed range of products rather than increasing the number of products.

Scaling Methods

While scaling your business, you will have the following possibilities to expand the business:

1. Distributors
2. Retail Stores
3. Showrooms/Sales Offices
4. Sales/Marketing Agents
5. Resellers
6. Existing groupings of people like schools, colleges and corporations
7. Online Shops
8. Online Resellers

Depending on your business, you will be able to use one or more of the above to scale your business. The above segments will be of help to you in scaling your business territorially. It is very important to choose the right partners, like distributors and resellers. Their efficiency and zeal will determine a lot about your business. In fact, at Appin, we always have to pre-select only positive and energetic partners. This is absolutely essential. You should try to achieve excellence in all ways but should adopt only a few partners in the beginning, to maintain the focus. Focus is the key to your business.

Human Resource

While scaling your business you will realise that now you must spend maximum time in planning and taking decisions. Thus, you will have a heavy requirement of people who will manage and execute everyday business. You will have to develop an assessment process to evaluate how people are performing. While scaling, you must always remember that you need to hire smart people, but at the same time hire the expertise that you require. This is very important. You will also understand that hiring is a process. You need to understand the employee retention cycle and then hire accordingly.

7

Human Resource Management

One of the most important parts of running an organisation is human resource management.

There are a few important points that must be kept in mind:

1. Human Resource is not a one-time job. It is a complete process and needs to be handled day-to-day. Always be on the look-out for hiring smart people and only smart people.
2. Human Resource means management of the complete workforce of the company, including you.
3. 90% of the people are not self-motivated. They need to be motivated and made accountable.
4. The complete team should be accountable and you should regularly check them for commitment, quality and hard work.
5. Don't base a resource on trust. Try to make it independent of trust. Award trustworthy people but don't base the system on trust.

6. It is very important to have standard policies for the whole company.
7. Train your workforce for your needs.

As Appin grew really fast, we didn't lay stress on Human Resource Management. We didn't follow many of the points mentioned above until we faced some serious problems. For example, one of our employees stole our Intellectual Property and parallel to his work at Appin, started another organisation. When we came to know about it, we were shocked and angry; more so because he was the first employee in the company. It was then that we realised our mistake of basing our HR system on trust.

From our experience in setting up a good team, we realised that generally it's only a few people who run an organisation: the rest just follow. It took us a while to accept this fact. You have to be among those few people. You have to be a part of the HR team to:

1. Motivate them
2. Understand them

3. Manage them
4. Train them
5. Listen to them

Until and unless you do the above, it is not possible to manage the entire employee force. It is very important to understand that human resource is a process and not a time-to-time activity. You should never be dependent on a person. Thus, it is very important to always be in the process of hiring. You can see this from a very common example. When you open the classified section in the papers, you will always see advertisements by the same companies week after week. Why so? This is because they are always in the process of hiring. If you don't follow this process, your organisation will face problems when people leave the company...and people *will* leave. Our organisation suffered losses of millions when certain key people left the company.

The other part of HR is management of the existing team. You need to regularly solve problems that the team faces regarding resources, their efficiency, etc. At Appin, we regularly have parties for good 'ol fun as well as understanding of the team. It is good to maintain the integrity and friendly environment in the company. In order to manage the time and results of your team well, you must first become a master of your own time. You need to manage your time and results in a smart way. Until and unless you can do that, it is impossible to do the same for your employees.

Accountability is very important in a company. Every team member needs to be held accountable; the success of your company depends on it. And you need to impress on them that they are not accountable to a single person or a team but to the whole company. It is also very important to understand that if someone is not accountable, it is your responsibility to make him/her accountable.

It is bound to develop trust on certain people and it is a good habit to trust people. However, you should make your processes such that they are independent of the trust. At Appin, we faced a lot of problems because many of our processes were based on trust. And what happens is that people tend to misuse that for their own personal benefits.

Also, you need to have a set of company work policies. It is important to standardise the working conditions of the whole team. You should discuss new policies with your team before enforcing them. The policies must be agreeable to everyone who joins the company. Exceptions can be raised and should be considered if logical.

Always train your team as per your company's vision. The training is not entirely work-related but is also related to the vision of the company. This will then reflect in the whole system. It is very important that your employees are aligned with the vision of the company.

In a nutshell, understand the importance of human resource, otherwise it may become the biggest danger for you.

8

Marketing Expertise

We have always believed in making the move and wisely so. Many times, we put too much into planning and don't take action. At any time in the business, momentum is very important. Our mentor Anthony Robbins speaks a lot on momentum. Well, that was the strength we had. We made a lot of moves which people did not expect us to. Marketing is one such aspect that requires momentum.

Many people define marketing in their own sense. Let us see a few definitions of marketing:

'Marketing is the means to make a communication about a product or service the purpose of which is to encourage recipients of the communication to purchase or use the product or service.'

'Marketing is the process of planning and executing the conception, pricing, promotion and distribution of ideas, goods and services to satisfy customers.'

Our mentor Philip Kotler defines marketing as 'knowing the customer and being an answer to his/her need that he/she understands clearly.'

When Appin began marketing, we all had a perception about our company. We always thought that our product was good and the customer base would react positively to it. We thought of certain aspects of packaging, but forgot many of them. When we did not get a positive reply from the customer, we would wonder why. We used to sit for hours trying to figure out where we lost. Sometimes we had the answer and sometimes we didn't, but we used to learn. We did not realise that we learnt more about the customer with every visit. And because of that, today we understand a lot about our customer base.

Innovative Concepts

Our journey of marketing began with very innovative concepts. We did not have the capital to print brochures or give advertisements. So we used our student network to market some initial programs. We tried what we call in technical terms "Buzz Marketing". We spread a roar among students about Appin and the workshops we were organising. We organised promotional seminars and used posters as a medium to publicise it. We remember making some of the best posters to market these workshops while at the same time, using our student network to spread the word about Appin. At that time Appin was just a founders' company with no employees. This was in its truest sense, one of the most innovative ways of marketing. The workshops went well but were not up to the students' expectations. Thus, it became very difficult to organise workshops in the same group.

Customer Satisfaction

With this we realised a very important point in marketing: it is not just about spreading an awareness of a solution for customer needs; it is also to meet those needs with satisfaction. One satisfied customer guarantees many more satisfied customers. However, a customer who is dissatisfied ensures that many customers are lost.

Surely everyone in a running business understands this, and so did we. However, in the beginning, it's possible to forget the importance of a satisfied customer. This will hurt your business badly. And so you must make it a point that no matter what, you will match your customer's expectations. This is necessary to move further ahead.

Marketing

Marketing is a very tricky process in a start-up. The following points can help a company in marketing:

- The age of the company
- Founders and promoters of the company
- Clarity of the product
- Right packaging
- Right price
- Right promotional strategy
- Valuable collaborations
- Excellent marketing material
- Make the move

Our company was founded by technical people. Hence, we didn't really have any experience of marketing. Although we had international marketing experience for a previous venture known as XIRs Ventures Inc. situated in Austin, Texas, USA, this was a different market. Thus, we needed to work hard for it. As for the factors above, we really didn't have any of the points apart from the last one, i.e., 'Make the move'. After all, it's an age-old saying that "The best way to learn swimming is to jump into the water." We started meeting the directors and deans of major institutes in our domain. They all started liking our concept but were doubtful of our capabilities. Of course, since we were students at the time, it was difficult for them to trust our capability.

In the meantime, with experience, we started getting better in all the above mentioned points. Influential people started becoming a part of our organisation, giving us a greater value. Though they were not a part of daily operations, their advice helped the company to work in a better way.

Thus, if you want to market in the best way, follow these points:

- Get key people as advisors
- Develop a pricing and promotional strategy
- Collaborate with companies that already have market reputation. Don't wait for this to happen but always stay in the hunt
- Have good and clear marketing material

In the initial times, a company is generally not confident about its product/services. In such a case, you often start over-promising the customer. Just note that over-promising and not delivering doesn't help much. Promise only those things that you are sure you can deliver. The best methodology is "Promise less, deliver more."

Marketing has a lot of dynamics associated with it. Thus it is very important to have an evaluation procedure for marketing. Of course, to evaluate marketing, it is very important to understand marketing of your company. So much so that one of the main founders should understand and be involved in it. We followed this approach and it proved to be really beneficial. As we understood a lot about our clients and their needs, it helped us in shaping the product in the same way.

For example, we discovered that the process of interacting with a new customer followed a certain methodology:

1. Developing rapport with the customer
2. Developing a positive image of the company in front of the customer
3. Showing the need to the customer
4. Showing how you are the best solution for his/her need
5. Final Closing

Many times, you might forget step 1 or step 2 and jump to step 3, or you may forget step 3, 4, 5. We need to understand that all five steps are important. Your company should have a methodology of following all the five steps whenever you are interacting with a new customer. This will help your organisation to form right websites, brochures, pitches, cold-calling statements, e-mails, etc. All the people interested in marketing should read more on use of NLP for marketing. NLP stands for Neuro Lingual Programming and is one of the latest techniques used in the area of marketing. It is very important that indirectly you must let your customers know about your achievements, expertise, etc.

It is said, "The best sales and marketing person is a very good listener." This is indeed true. Always be a good listener to your customer. Sometimes, customers used to bring in their complaints to our offices. It was important that we listened to the customer and understood his/her problem. Thus, we adopted a very customer-centric focus. Our Brand Manager used to make sure this was implemented. One of the key statements that suitably fit here is, *"Your customer is the person who is responsible for giving bread and butter to your company. Treat him accordingly."* It is also very important that everyone doesn't get involved in solving a customer's problem, otherwise your organisation might lose focus.

Innovative Marketing Methods

In a start-up, it is very difficult to adopt the conventional methods of marketing. You need huge financial backup to follow the conventional methods of marketing. You need to adopt innovative new methods and also make a marketing plan. By marketing plan, we don't mean an excel chart with exponentially growing revenues in subsequent years. That is only good for winning business plan competitions. In reality, you need to decide how many hours you and your company will dedicate to marketing as well as how much money you can shell out for it. Keep it very simple. Then, in the next stage, you may plan the activities that are possible with the given budget and man-hours. Most start-ups face the problem of over-predicting, because they never plan. We also faced this problem and learnt the hard way. This is very important and will help you to structure and scale marketing activities later on.

However, keep one thing in mind. Try out new things and take risks. Every mistake that you make will be a new learning. Just make sure that you are doing it in a planned manner so that it doesn't affect the company very badly. This means taking only those risks which can be taken by your company financially.

Product-Customer Quadrant

The Product-Customer quadrant understanding is very important. Whenever a company has to plan for the coming time, it should understand the product-customer quadrant. Here is a very simple diagram that shows the quadrant:

New Product Existing Customer (Quadrant 3)	New Product New Customer (Quadrant 4)
Existing Product Existing Customer (Quadrant 1)	Existing Product New Customer (Quadrant 2)

The diagram has four quadrants. Quadrant 1 represents the strategy you follow when marketing the existing product to the existing customer.

Similarly, Quadrant 2 represents a strategy when you market an existing product to a new customer. This means that you are scouting for a new customer.

Quadrant 3 represents a strategy when you market a new product to an existing customer. This means you are creating a new product and marketing to an existing customer. This is called 'cross selling'.

Finally, Quadrant 4 represents a strategy when you market a new product to a new customer. This means that you are creating a new product and targeting it to a new customer. This happens a lot in a start-up company, and is the major reason for the loss of focus.

It has been observed that most of the start-up companies unconsciously spend a lot of time in Quadrant 4, which is very dangerous for their business. We did not realise this until a very good friend and a mentor Pradeep Chopra, the co-founder of Whizlabs, pointed this out to us. Since then, we have been trying to stay away as much as possible from the 4th quadrant. Being in all the other quadrants is just a matter of strategy.

Essentials of Marketing

Marketing is as important for a start-up as it is for an established company. In fact, it is the most crucial issue, since the objectives of going into business need to be conveyed to the target customer even before the products are ready. Here are some of the basic things to be kept in mind:

Knowing the Customer

Our friend Nikhil Rasiwasia had a wonderful idea of providing some niche computer courses for school students. He was absolutely sure that students would love to have these courses. He went and tried to convince some schools about these courses but didn't succeed. Getting frustrated, he asked one day, "I am sure that this is a wonderful thing for the students. Then why is it that I am not able to sell it to them?" We understood his concern and answered, "The courses are good for the students and you are marketing to the school. Why will they buy it? First identify your customer. School is a different customer altogether, so you need to prepare a different strategy for schools." In a nutshell, you must understand whom are you marketing your product to.

The Product

It needs to be a customer-centric product with clear USPs (Unique Selling Propositions). A good mantra is, "Don't invent and modify the product with your beliefs; do it with customer's beliefs." A quality product with clear-cut benefits to the customer is very important. For example, in the case mentioned above, Nikhil should have made a proposal offering revenue-sharing models and certain other benefits to the school. This would have offered a clear-cut benefit to the school.

The Pricing

This is a very important factor in marketing. There are many ways to price your product. One is customer-centric pricing. This follows the methodology of asking how much the customer is ready to pay for products and services closest to yours. You may also take out this information from surveys but experience says that people rarely fill surveys like these seriously. Once, we were conducting a seminar for IT professionals. We distributed a survey form which had a question, "How much would you like to pay for seminars related to this one?" The options were a) $20, b) $40, c) $80. Most of the people chose the first option. The irony was that they had paid $80 to attend this seminar. Thus, a study of competitor's products and services is a good way. It also depends a lot on your strategy. If you want to reach more customers you will price the product low, and if vice versa, you will price the product higher. There is also another way to price the product. You may calculate the cost of the product, add your profit and launch it in the market. The problem here is that in a start-up, it is very difficult to focus on actual costs.

The Promotional Methods

It is very important to use the promotional methods in tandem with the strategy you adopt. For example, if your product has students as end customers then radio, school/college festivals and the like may be a good way to promote your product. However, if your customer is the school itself, then it is better to sponsor school authorities' meets, newsletters, conferences, etc. Some of the commonly used promotional methods are:

- Print Media – It is one of the more expensive means of marketing. It is mainly used for the development of a brand. It is a very good medium to find business associates and maintaining a brand. It is very important to consistently be in the media.
- Posters/Pamphlets – If your business has an individual as a customer, this is a very good means to create awareness. It is a low cost method and commonly used by start-ups.
- Radio – It is a very effective medium to reach the common man. Again, like print media, it needs to be consistent and innovative.

- Television – One of the most expensive means of promotion, but with the widest reach, it is generally good for businesses with huge funds and products for everyday customers. This is used primarily for branding purposes.
- Sponsorships – Sponsoring events relevant to your domain is a good way to promote your company. This is a widely accepted practice.
- Promotional Seminars – A very important way to create awareness about your product. You may organise these seminars at key places. If you are able to put some intellect into the seminars, you may even organise them for free or charge for them.
- Sales Force – A dedicated sales force directly going to the customers is one of the common ways of promoting your product. You need to train your sales force and set up effective channels for analysing their performance.
- Internet Marketing – This is one of the most innovative ways to promote your product. There are various possibilities in Internet marketing. These include e-mail campaigns, website search engine optimisations, reverse linking websites with relevant websites, submission to various search engines and directories on the Internet, Google Adwords campaign, Yahoo search marketing and resellers on the Internet. This is the most cost-effective way of promoting your product and has a worldwide audience. There are a number of huge resellers on the Internet like eBay, Amazon, etc.
- Surface Mail Campaign – This requires sending surface mailers to your existing database regarding your product/service.
- Distributors/Franchisees – This is a very important method of scaling your business and playing a volumes

game. At the same time, this is a very tricky process and requires expertise. When Appin went in for channel partners, we had to plan and make variations in the product for around six months prior to launching the scheme.

Database Development

This is one of the most important jobs of the marketing team. The biggest asset most of the businesses have is database. Many companies are bought by big giants because they have huge databases. Every company should have a focus on developing a customer database with as much information about the customer as they may require. This data can be used to market and cross sell your products. At any point of time, do not forget the importance of the development of a database in any business. Big internet giants like Yahoo, Google, etc., have databases as their biggest assets.

Development of a Brochure

A brochure needs to be developed for the following purposes:

- Give an outlook to your company – This essentially means that the customers should be so mesmerised by the design and overall get-up of the brochure that they feel that the company is professional.
- Briefing about the company and its advantages like infrastructure, people, technology, etc.
- Identification of the need and explaining how your product can be a solution to meet the customer's needs.
- Testimonials and case studies to prove that you have been successful in implementing the solutions.
- Contact information, so that the customer can contact you in any way possible like e-mail, website, postal address, office phone number, SMS number, etc.

Development of a Website

We are living in the IT age and it is very important to host a fully functional website. The website should at least have the following features:

- About the company with brochure downloads
- Clients
- Products with brochure downloads
- Media coverage
- Case studies
- Free resources
- Contact information/form

Suggested Additional Features:

- Blogs
- Recommended links
- Online customer support
- E-commerce pages, if required

In today's world, a website plays a very important role in the branding and marketing of a company. It's important that your company website lives up to the expectations of your customers.

Development of an Effective Sales/Customer Interaction Team

This is an extremely important aspect. The job of the sales team is to capitalise on the marketing and branding efforts and close the deal. It is very important to develop an effective sales/customer interaction team as they are the public face of the company and are responsible for setting an image of the company in front of the customers. You should make sure that the team has values aligned with the company's policy. One of my associates Ruchi Gupta said, "The marketing person is the company for the customer." In fact, one of our Directors from

USA, Anuj Khare, happens to be an expert in training sales teams. He is an NLP specialist and motivator who can transform your whole sales team. He literally transformed our team in sales and customer interaction.

Coming from the past experiences of marketing, a new product generally starts getting a response only three months after its rigorous marketing begins. Marketing also tends to highlight areas where major improvements are required in your products and services. Thus, marketing is a very important part of any business. You should take it very seriously, because it is the marketing strategies that create the image of your company in the eyes of the world.

9

Brand Development and Management

One of the most complete definitions of a Brand goes like this: "A brand is the symbolic embodiment of all the information connected with a product or service." A brand typically includes a name, logo, and other visual elements such as images or symbols. It also encompasses the set of expectations associated with a product or service which typically arise in the minds of people. Such people include employees of the brand owner, people involved with distribution, sale or supply of the product or service, and ultimate consumers.

Even while writing this chapter, we remember the day in the year 2004, when Divya Laul, our President, Brand Management, made three of the co-founders sit together during a hectic day at office. Then she started playing a game with us. She asked us to say the first thought which came into our minds when she would say a word. These were the results of the game:

Word (by Divya)	Co-Founder 1	Co-Founder 2	Co-Founder 3
Coke	Always Coca Cola	Best soft drink	Coca-Cola
Mercedes	Big Car	Luxury	Luxury
Nike	Just do it	Just do it	Just do it
PVR	Multiplex	Movies	Movies and fun
Appin	________	Courses	________

Two of us had surprised looks on our faces when she said "Appin", while the third one said "Courses".

Recapping the whole story, after the initial hesitation of playing the game and warming up with the words "Coke" and "Mercedes", we were actually enjoying the game. Nike and PVR happened next and then came Appin. Somewhere inside, we knew that she would ask us Appin for sure, but then when it actually came as the fifth word, we were taken by surprise. What was more surprising was that two of us actually had no answer to it, while one of us said "Courses". This is where she stopped the game and asked us "Hey guys, what *do* you really want from Appin Knowledge Solutions?"

That day really changed our perception towards branding. Two weeks later, our branding team headed by Divya came out with the tagline "Discover Technology, the Right Way!" That is what we do. We help students, corporates and academia discover technology the right way using innovative, yet simplified methods. Today, if she would play the game, we would say Appin is associated with "Niche, project-based, job-oriented courses." This is the perception that we have created in the minds of our customers and it persists till today. When we look back on that day, we really thank her for taking us through that simple yet effective exercise.

Today, businesses have new and more effective ways of increasing brand awareness and more importantly, creating brand loyalty. One of the most important tasks involved in ensuring a brand's success, is to develop an effective branding strategy.

You will need to position your brand over the potential competitors or your existing competitors. You will have to fight to get their customer base and also protect your own customer base from them. You might be the first in your field. The first mover advantage will initially give you an edge to establish your brand in an efficient manner. However, the honeymoon will not last long, as competition is bound to arrive sooner than later. You will need to develop a brand proposition, which, when conveyed in marketing and advertising campaigns, will provide a simple yet attractive, unique and relevant message to past, present and potential customers. The same proposition will also need to be engaged in the whole human resource of your company including the senior executives, customer support executives, marketing and sales team, product development teams and strategic partners.

Today, branding is a combination of advertising and public relations. People do not easily believe the ads they see on television, newspapers or hear on the radio. It would require an expensive advertising campaign to make people familiar with your brand. However, public relations is not the same. If you can use PR properly to do branding for you, it will work out cheaper and will be much more effective. Contact the journalist of the target customer's most likely read newspaper and impress upon him or her, the idea or product. If it is good, it will make way for itself to the newspaper. That article will be coming from a neutral source and will be read by your potential customers who will actually start recognising your brand. The same also applies for other media such as television or radio. Also, as a start-up, you might not even have enough resources to go in for an advertisement campaign in the beginning. On the contrary, as your company grows, you will learn how to use PR more effectively. This would be a good time to start actively putting in a budget for advertising campaigns.

Branding is all about an experience which will be attached to your product or service. One way would be that you let your customer make his or her own choices and experiences. The other would be that you take control of the whole experience. Those who have gone ahead to use the power of branding to create a whole customer experience have made loyal, diehard fans out of their customers for their products and services.

Why is Everyone Talking of Branding?

Every time your customer will use your product or service, there will be an experience attached to it. Now, either the customer will make his own experience or you can help him experience one. This is the power of branding. You have to ensure that his experience is good. Starbucks gave coffee lovers an experience to talk about. Harley-Davidson did the same with bike fans. Appin gives its customers an experience of discovering technology in the right way.

But why Branding?

It is important to realise why branding is so crucial in today's time. This is especially important for a start-up as you will have an opportunity to create the brand for your product or service from Day One itself. This will help you create a strong hold in the market.

Branding will help in giving you a sustained advantage over your competitors. As the customer will finally choose to buy one of the products, if you create a clear brand perception in his mind, your chances of winning him over are maximum. He will fall in love with the product.

How do You Develop the Brand?

The first step is to identify what the core values for your business are. For some it might be honesty and client satisfaction, for others it might be customer service. Appin's core values are the quality of its courses and the comfort in which a participant does a course.

Everything that you do with your business should reflect the core values that you stand for. Although you may not directly go and proclaim these values, they will be broadcast to your target segment through all your actions. These values form the heart of your brand and should remain consistent over time.

Select Your Audience Carefully

You could be making a product which might suit only a higher income group. In such a case, you might not consider branding your product with anything to do with a railway station. You would rather go to an airport and advertise there!

You might consider some of these key points in selecting and understanding your audience:

1. Composition of the target audience
2. Needs of the target audience
3. Desires of the target audience
4. Role of your product and service in serving the needs and the desires of the consumers
5. Advantages over any pre-existing competition
6. Price comparison – justification in all three cases – lower, higher or similar price

Developing a Brand Statement
(Brand Proposition)

Brand Proposition is the central promise a brand makes to its consumers. The brand proposition must be appealing, easily understood and relevant to the target market. Truly understanding your target audience, in addition to having a realistic assessment of what your product offers, is invaluable in assisting you in the development of a successful brand proposition.

We have created an effective brand for our technology courses at Appin Knowledge Solutions. We deliver to our customers only "Niche, project-based, job-oriented courses". Every word here gives out a clear meaning to our target audience.

Niche means that we deal in only high-end technologies. And only those who are passionate about technology and want to gain new and the latest skills would want to do our courses.

Project-based means that our courses are based on projects and give a lot of hands-on experience.

Job-oriented means that after doing our courses, there will be an actual value-addition to your skills which will help you get a better and more satisfying job in the industry.

Always Keep a Promise

It's always nice to promise heaven in your brand proposition to get the target audience to try out your product or service.

However, the honeymoon period will not last very long if the promise is not fulfilled. Following through with an excellent product/service and customer support will put an unforgettable mark in the memory of your existing customers. This will create brand loyalty and take your brand through good and bad times.

A brand that has high familiarity but low likeability is heading for trouble as it has not been able to fulfil its promises after actually reaching its target audience successfully. Such a brand will slip from its place and finally disappear from the minds of the customers.

A brand that has high likeability but low familiarity will have a high potential to expand. This is the one which has been able to deliver its promise and is now ready to be known to a larger domain of its target audience.

Be Their Life-long Friend

An important aspect of brand development is to create a positive emotional attachment to the brand which creates a response in its audience without the audience seeing the product or directly experiencing the service. Thinking about 'Fed-Ex', you will feel that your courier will definitely reach on time and safely to its destination. This is a feeling of trust that the brand 'Fed-Ex' has developed in you. Similarly, thinking of Appin evokes a response of latest technologies being learnt in a way which is innovative and creative.

If you are able to create this emotional attachment for your customer with your brand, not only have you made him your customer for life, but he will also get you new customers. And his words will matter more than any advertisement or press release.

Such an attachment is a result of a mutually beneficial relationship between your customer and the company. Be sure to take feedback from your customer, and tell him that his views really matter to you. Change according to the current needs and desires of the customer, and let the customer know that you really care for his/her suggestions which, in turn, help you to bring about the changes.

This may be the most difficult and often overlooked aspect of successful brand development. This is also where a lack of comprehensive research into identifying the target audience's needs and desires can either make or break an attempt at developing a positive emotional attachment between the brand and its audience. If not done effectively, a seemingly insurmountable communication gap will develop between the internal brand perception and the audience's actual perception.

> **Strong Brand = Product Benefits × Distinct Identity × Emotional Values**
>
> –Peter Doyle,
> *Marketing Management & Strategy*, 1997

Part - II

Our Own Story

(December 23rd 2003, 9:15 p.m.)

"I want to do something exciting in the coming semester," said Ankur Gupta, a 3rd year electrical engineering student from IIT Bombay.

Sitting in Dominos at Kamla Nagar in Delhi were four friends who were meeting after a gap of six months, after a hectic semester of their engineering course. They were enjoying freshly baked pizzas that were exceptionally welcome, given the chilly weather conditions outside.

"I have an idea," said Nikhil, an extremely tall vegetarian with an appetite large enough to beat hollow that of a person thrice his weight! Also pursuing a degree in electrical engineering, but from IIT Kanpur, Nikhil was popularly known as Nikux in his hostel. All his hometown friends had also taken a fancy to the name. An intellectual – in fact, a genius intellectually – Nikux was unofficially called the "designer man" of his college; he was a master of CorelDRAW and Adobe Photoshop, software names that any computer geek is familiar with.

"Tell me about it," said Ankur excitedly. It was all the prodding that Nikhil needed to continue. "Last semester, my friend and roomie Saurabh and I thought of imparting computer knowledge to school students. But the idea failed. We had an impeccable presentation, solid idea and a technically qualified team. We went to various schools all over Kanpur to sell the courses to the principals. They were even interested."

"Apart from the pricing being good, our courses were designed in such a way that they would not disturb the school curriculum. These courses would add to the students' knowledge immensely, and be very useful to them in later experimentation," explained Nikhil.

Rajat enjoyed good food, and had so far remained silent. But now he was listening intently. Rajat was pursuing a degree in computer science from IIT Delhi, and was the highest IIT-JEE ranker amongst them. Now, his eager curiosity got the better of him: "What happened then?" he blurted out impatiently.

"And why didn't we hear about it during the semester?" asked Ishan. Ishan was pursuing his degree in instrumentation and control engineering from Delhi Institute of Technology, better known nowadays as the Netaji Subhas Institute of Technology, Delhi. He had managed to demolish more than half his pizza; he wasn't the type to let anything or anyone disturb his concentration when it came to food! But Nikhil's admission that he had failed in something, had taken him by surprise. Ishan knew that Nikhil was not a man to give up on a good idea easily. 'What,' wondered Ishan, 'could have gone so terribly wrong as to make someone like Nikhil admit defeat?'

Nikhil knew this was coming and probably had the answer ready in his mind. "When we went to the principals of various schools, they all loved the idea. But they all asked one question to which we had no answer."

"And that was…?" urged Ishan.

"What every principal wanted to know was: 'If my students are scoring high marks in boards and passing with flying colours, why on earth would I be interested in taking your courses? What possible benefit could be derived from them?'" said Nikhil while making a gesture with his hand – the same one that probably seven out of ten principals would have made while asking this question.

"Where's my pizza?" yelled a voice from the entrance. None of them turned around. They knew who it was. They also knew that he would have parked his car on the wrong side of the road, making it an easy target for the tow truck.

"Ishan, did you just eat the whole pizza by yourself? Where's my Spicy Chicken?"

"It wasn't all that spicy today, so I thought you wouldn't like it and ate it myself. I was actually doing you a favour," said Ishan.

Tarun lived closest to this Dominos outlet and thus felt that he would take the least time to reach. It was just that he started a little late and as usual left the keys inside the car! Pursuing his engineering degree from Bharti Vidyapeeth, Delhi, in electronics and communication, he always blamed Ishan for finishing his share of the food.

"Order something for me and tell me what's happening."

"Nikhil was telling us about an idea that had come to him when he was in Kanpur; it seems he wasn't in a position just then to implement it successfully. But what he's been telling us is very interesting. Maybe we can do something about it," said Ishan.

"I've been giving it a good amount of thought myself for some days now," confessed Ishan. "We all realise that there's something missing from our educational system. The practical aspect is just not there. Are students who pass out of technical educational institutions *really* ready for stepping into the industry? Why don't we do something that can help students like us understand their subjects from a more practical viewpoint? This would equip them to really contribute to the industry from Day One: land on their feet running, so to speak. We could do something concrete, like giving courses or workshops on various technologies to students," added Ishan enthusiastically.

Rajat – who'd had a distant look in eyes all this time – was now brimming with excitement. Ishan knew from experience that his mind had been racing with ideas and he was about to say something really significant. "Let's get together and help the students. Let's give the students what they want and see how well we can give it to them. Let's start something that will not only change *their* lives but *our* lives too…forever. Half of our college life is over, and we still haven't done anything that would set us apart from the others. But now, something tells me that our time has come. Ankur, exciting times will be here soon."

Ishan leapt to his feet and said, "Let's bridge the gap."

Tarun looked up and mused, "How come my car is moving? Oh *NO*! It's getting towed away!" he wailed. "WAIT! *STOP!*" he yelled as he chased it down the street…

A summary of events that followed that chilly Delhi night…

After dinner that night, we went into a huddle for two consecutive days, brainstorming and discussing all the aspects of our idea. It began from the concept of "bridging the gap". We always believed that our education at school could have been better in many ways; this applied equally to the education provided in colleges. And thus the vision evolved. After a lot of thinking, it was decided that the nascent company's name would be APPIN. At the same time, the team decided to target schools as well as colleges in niche technology areas. Ishan and Rajat accelerated the process by getting everyone's signatures on a partnership deed and opening a bank account.

They organised a few seminars and workshops to begin with, along with Tarun. Nikhil developed the website and looked after poster designing. After the grand success of the workshops, the company's activities came to a temporary halt because of the impending examinations of its founders. Moreover, apart from Rajat and Tarun, the others had commitments of internships that kept them busy. However, they were bonded together and with the support of the team, Rajat and Tarun marketed the first big deal of Appin. They were fully supported by the rest including their sixth partner, Aman who – since he had other plans in life – went his separate way soon after, as did Nikhil.

Rajat's elder brother Anuj used to mentor the team. He was in the United States but stayed in regular touch via e-mails and phone calls. He was already an entrepreneur and his experience helped the team to perform better and better. However, without the founders having an iota of experience in the entrepreneurial world, all of them being from a technical background, they had obvious limitations. They never focussed on the cash flows, processes and formal methodology of marketing. On the other hand, their capacity for hard work was tremendous. All of them were committed to the venture and started conducting training programs in Delhi, Kanpur, Mumbai, Pune and Chennai. Budding students in various regions supported the venture. Nipun and Varun were two such students. Varun turned out to be an exceptional asset to the company and played an important role in setting it up in South India. In the meantime, Appin also recruited some trainers and back office support, the primary ones being Anup, the chief technology engineer and Narendra, without whom the office would not have been able to function. Anup had a lot of experience in the training industry and Narendra's back-end support made him an invaluable, irreplaceable asset.

It was a time when the company didn't have enough training programs and hence the workforce was relatively free. One day, Rajat had the brainwave that since the trainers were free much of the time, why not have them develop some innovative learning material in hi-end technologies. None of them could ever have imagined that this (HomTech) idea would snowball and become one of the most famous products in the training industry.

In the meantime, Anuj took a bold decision to move to India for a while and help the organisation grow and realise its true potential. He was a well-known 'Success Psychology' coach trained in USA by professionals like Anthony Robbins, Deepak Chopra and many others. Under his guidance, the company grew tremendously. Soon, along came Ruchi, another reinforcement in marketing. With her self-motivation, dedication and guidance to the whole team, the company moved into a new office, and a new Appin began to take shape from April 2005.

On account of there being large number of colleges as clients, the workforce grew to over 30. The operations were managed well by Anuj and Tarun, while the marketing was handled by Ishan, Rajat and Ruchi. Being the senior-most in the trainer's team, Anup trained the team on how to conduct training programs. Appin was always known for niche technology programs all over its territories. However, the founders wanted to raise the quality of service to another level.

Rajat had worked internationally: in Europe, Singapore and also with many upcoming technical start-ups in India and USA. Nikhil also had international experience and had worked with a company known as Kalzoom Technologies. Ishan possessed the skills of a shrewd business person, and his international exposure and college activities were of great help to him and the team. Tarun had expertise in online businesses and selling. Anuj was the matured energy of Appin with a mixture of experience, energy and the ability to motivate and channelise the company's energy. In fact, the Appin team were well positioned for global selling because its founders were globally oriented and were from leading institutions of India.

Ankur left the company after a while on account of personal reasons, leaving Appin totally in the hands of Ishan, Tarun, Rajat and Anuj. The quartet used to discuss and plan a lot of things together. Ishan's college friends Ankur Jain and Ankur Bansal had helped Appin a lot. Mayank and Jitin, who stayed with Appin through thick and thin, made significant contributions. Jitin was one of the main technical brains of Appin and was responsible for setting up the technical aspects. Mayank was a street-smart guy and helped Appin in lots of processes with impressive results. The company was further strengthened by the coming of Vipin, who left a secure job at Honda to lend a shoulder to Appin. He started improving the quality of Appin products, and also subtly tightened up discipline within the company.

Our branding head, Divya, was another one who played a significant role in the company. It was she who brought brand awareness to the team. She gave the company one of its famous taglines, "Discover technology, the right way". She later played an even more instrumental role in branding related activities of Appin. She did not come from a technology background, and that helped a lot. She invariably came up with a viewpoint that was quite different from the rest of the team, who were all from the same technology background. This really helped to understand Appin's customers better.

Very soon, Appin's primary product started selling all over the globe, with resellers and Appin international websites. Covering the Singapore and Philippines markets further accelerated Appin's expansion. This was followed by another giant stride: launching Appin Technology Labs in various parts of India. Rajat and Mr. Sheshadri, a venture capitalist from

Chennai, closed the first deal of Appin Technology Labs. Mr. Sheshadri helped the company in realising its business model and in taking the company's activities into different regions.

This is the true story of the evolution of Appin, right from the germination of the idea from a concept realised by student entrepreneurs, well-supported by successful alumni like Mr. Vishnu Dusad, CMD of Nucleus Software, Dr. Dheeraj Bhardwaj of IIT Delhi, Prof. SK Gupta of IIT Delhi, Mr. Ashok Sapra, Managing Director of AT&T and the Chairman and quality assurance brain of Appin, Mr. AS Chandrasekhar, popularly known as "Uncle" among the Appin founders. Partner companies like Whizlabs, Kritikal Solutions, Virtualwire Technologies and Microsoft Corporation also helped Appin. Kapil and Pradeep of Whizlabs steered the company in an appropriate direction.

During this course, the company had its share of ups and downs, including lots of clashes among the founders. But the team surged strongly through these squalls, emerging even more closely knit than before, and very proud to be known as 'Team Appin'. The company has already contributed to the lives of students and professionals all over the globe, and plans to expand more extensively in the coming years.

Part - III

Those who 'Made the Move'

Experience Cannot be Taught

—By Ambika Pillai

Growing up in the south during the '60s taught me that being true to yourself is the only real road to happiness and fulfilment. As luck would have it, I never really found my groove till pretty late in life.

I've come to believe there are two kinds of people: people who are born talented and the others who work and strive very hard to learn and master an art. I know now that I've been blessed with an art which has won me many awards and has been appreciated by thousands. I thank God for keeping an eye out for me.

I have never been professionally trained in make-up, though I *did* go to school for hairdressing. I chanced on make-up purely by default. I believe in every field you need a godfather, and mine was Hemant Trivedi. A perfectionist himself, he recognised my hidden talent and gave me the biggest break of my career. I was barely two faces old when he got me to do the then reigning Miss World Aishwarya Rai's face for an ad film which won me the *Best Make-up Artist of the Year* award. There's been no looking back since.

I have come to realise that rules – and words like "Never" and "Always" – are sure death to creativity. I am grateful for my lack of formal training in make-up. The journey itself may have taken longer, but along the way I discovered things I could not have been 'taught'. For me, new and exciting ideas are most often created when chances are taken and rules are broken.

I have been in this field for 18 long years, out of which 8 years were spent hopping from one salon to another as a hair stylist. It's been 10 years since ***Ambika Pillai*** opened. The journey has been long and gruelling, but hard work eventually pays off. What started with one salon and 8 employees has expanded into 4 salons with 200 employees. Today, I see myself as a gratified woman in a rewarding job!

Ambika Pillai is known as the 'Make-up artiste with the Midas touch'. She is the owner of a chain of beauty salons all over India, famously known by the brand-name – 'Ambika Pillai' – She has won the 'Make-up Artist of the Year' award, from the Indian Academy of Advertising and Film Art.

Entrepreneurship is the Way to Live

— By Anuj Khare

It was the year 2000. This was my first week at the Master's program at University of Texas, Austin. My professor told me that there was a lecture where Dr. Dijkstras of Dijkstras algorithm fame was coming. I went to the lecture, where I happened to meet a graduate of UT Austin named Sandeep. He had recently graduated and set up a company that dealt with something to do with wireless. I was standing at the water fountain and trying to figure out how to use it. This was my first time in the US. He decided to come over and help me out.

Sandeep: "You new?"

Anuj: "Yes."

Sandeep: "Where do you come from?"

Anuj: "From IIT Delhi" (proud of his college)

He was not impressed.

Sandeep: "Do you have a specific reason for coming to UT?"

Anuj: "Yes. I wish to be an entrepreneur and set up my company here in college itself. The US is *the* land of opportunity and that's why I come here."

He smiled.

Sandeep: "What does being an entrepreneur mean to you?"

That set me thinking. I wasn't able to answer the question at that time. What did being an entrepreneur really mean to me? I knew it wasn't about money as probabilistically speaking, I had more chances of making money working for a Fortune 500 company than running a company. I knew that 9 of 10 businesses fail. Fame was also not the reason as I thought it's easier for writers to achieve that goal. Maybe I associated being my own boss with glamour, but then I knew it would be hard work. I didn't have an answer at that time.

I got a little engrossed with studies in my first semester, but the thought of becoming an entrepreneur still kept haunting me. I did try to justify my entrepreneurship desires. What did it really mean to me? Was it my way of giving back to the society, to the world? As true as that statement may be, it wasn't a big enough motivating factor for me. I dug further in my consciousness. The answer that came was simple and made a lot of sense. The very thought of running a corporation gave me juice. I knew that it would make me get up every morning and think about how my decisions today would lead to the betterment of the world. I feel that it was why I was born, I live and it is what I will die for.

As trite as it may sound, I truly believed in it then, and my views have only strengthened with time. Entrepreneurship is really a way to live; it is something which I want to be known for. Life without struggle or challenges is no life at all and I refuse to give in to the 9 to 5 job (good job) syndrome, to dictate my life. I wished to make all possible efforts to break the mould. The journey sounded more exciting to me than the destination.

And it was with this fire that my first company XIRS Ventures Inc was born in Austin, Texas, in the year 2001. The company was into innovative search solutions on XML documents, on the lines of Google for the web. When I look back now, I enjoy and cherish every moment I have spent for XIRS, but it was a hard decision when Rajat, co-author of this book along with Ishan, invited me to join Appin in 2004. It didn't mean I had to quit XIRS, but it did mean that a significant time would be taken off my plate.

That's when I learnt an important lesson about being opportunistic; I realised that the education market was growing at a much more rapid pace as compared to our shrinking margins in XIRS. I gladly accepted the offer. And in just 2 years' time, Appin had unprecedented growth where it reached 3 continents and established its presence as a world leader in onsite and distance learning courses in niche technology areas including nanotechnology, security and hacking, .NET and Robot-making using embedded systems, among others. I realised that we had achieved so much in so little time with sheer momentum; brute force and hard work do play an important role, contrary to what books may say when growing a business. The growth of an industry also plays a very important role, and it's probably more important to catch the right wave than doing things right.

As a core part of the senior management team at Appin Group of Companies, I congratulate Ishan and Rajat in coming up with this book to help fellow entrepreneurs. Appin would not be where it is today had it not been for them having the vision in their third year of engineering undergraduate program. As opposed to many authors who write on the subject of entrepreneurship, I identify them as *real* entrepreneurs from head to toe, who sleep, eat and drink the principles and advice mentioned in this book, and it's their labour of love that gives me confidence to refer to them as the 'youngest entrepreneurs of the century'.

As a message to the readers of this book, I will narrate a story I heard from the mythology *guru*, Joseph Campbell.

'Yseult was engaged to marry King Mark whom she had never seen. Mark sends Tristan to fetch Yseult for him. Yseult's mother prepares a love potion so that the two who are to be married will have love for each other. Tristan and Yseult inadvertently drink the love potion thinking it to be wine. After drinking the love potion, they are overcome by love. But Yseult's nurse realises what had happened and tells Tristan that they have drunk their death.

To this, Tristan says, "If, by my death, you mean this agony of love, then that is my life. If, by death, you mean the punishment we are to suffer if discovered, which means execution, I accept that. But if, by my death, you mean burning in the eternal fires of hell," (something which people in the Middle Ages literally believed to be true) "I accept that, too."

He was trying to say is that love is even bigger than death, than pain, than anything. This is the affirmation of the pain of life in a big way.

This story not only applies to love, but to entrepreneurship as well. Any life career that you choose in following your bliss should be chosen with the sense that no setback, no obstacle and no failure can scare you off. This journey is about enjoying these failures; it won't be possible but for these failures.

Anuj Khare is on the Board of Directors, Appin Group of Companies and Chairman, XIRS Ventures Inc. USA. He is a graduate from Indian Institute of Technology, Delhi, and has a Master's degree from the University of Austin, Texas. He is a prolific writer and has to his credit the books, "Psychology of Success in IIT-JEE" and "Science of Achievement". He has also been featured among the top motivational gurus of India by "The Week" magazine in 2006.

Follow Your Instincts

— *By Arjun Malhotra*

What makes a person a successful entrepreneur? I have often been asked this question. My answer, at the cost of sounding clichéd, is: an unquenchable zeal to act on your passions, and sustained belief in yourself.

Thirty years ago, when there was hardly any sign of the burgeoning growth of the IT industry in this country, six of us took a decision that most of our friends and relatives termed as "brave, but not necessarily intelligent". We left an organisation that was doing exceptionally well, and plunged into the uncertain world of adventure and entrepreneurship,

In the '70s, the decision to leave a company like DCM and start a company from a roof-top *barsati* (equivalent to the Silicon valley garages) was "brave", by all means. The capital deployed was a mere Rs.175,000, or $4,000 at current exchange rates. But the seeds we sowed have become the dynamic HCL Group, a 30,000 strong, $3 billion group with a presence in almost all continents.

Mere statistics can't begin to tell the entire story – of industry creation, market creation, and market expansion. Of technology change, of technology acquisition and product development. Of cannibalising successful products and businesses, of repeatedly gutting a powerful delivery organisation and rebuilding it for emerging opportunities. Of seeing rare skills becoming obsolete, and proactively re-skilling highly intelligent persons to address new challenges. Of new paradigm recognition, creation, development and refinement, separately for the Indian and global environments.

Case studies have been written about HCL's transitions, including one by HBS when software outsourcing began, way back in 1996. The pioneering, the strategisation, the rapid re-invention are still fresh in our minds. The successes and failures are the elements of de-risking for future endeavours. After my tryst with HCL for more than 20 years, I started TechSpan in late 1998 with funding from Goldman Sachs and Walden International. TechSpan was later merged with Headstrong in November 2003.

It was tough to leave an organisation, particularly one you have started and have grown. It also involved the risk of starting things from scratch. But I decided to follow my instincts once again.

Success in a venture, however, demands things other than your instinctive ideas. It requires extensive research, meticulous planning and thorough implementation.

Therefore, before taking a conclusive decision you must find answers, honest and unbiased, to the following questions:

1. How much faith do you have in yourself?
2. Do you have a vision in life?
3. How much risk can you take?

Three steps I suggest to budding entrepreneurs in starting their own business are:

1. Get some experience: It always helps. Experience helps get clarity of thought and in finding the right direction.
2. Find a passion: You will be happy only when you are passionate with your work and enjoy it.
3. Build a team: A well-knit team is crucial for the growth and development of an organisation. Two minds work better and faster than one, as they say.

Fundamentals for success for any entrepreneur, I would summarise as the answers to a few basic questions; get these right and success will be yours:

1. Why will someone buy your product? What benefit are you going to deliver to him?

2. Who will be your stakeholders? What value are you going to deliver to each one of them?
3. What value are you personally going to deliver to the entire enterprise? How will you justify your continued inclusion in it?

And, the most important one to you personally: does this picture generate passion in you…the passion to continue with it through thick and thin, persisting through adversity to find the answers and come out on top?

The final ingredients of success are, however, commitment and dedication. Unless you have an unwavering focus on your goals and you work hard (I mean ***hard***), your passion will fall flat on the ground.

Arjun Malhotra catalysed the birth and growth of the Indian InfoTech industry. Frontline in the creation and growth of the $20 billion Indian IT industry, he is Chief Executive Officer and Chairman of Headstrong's Board of Directors. Co-founder of HCL, one of India's first and largest Information Technology corporations, Arjun is one of India's foremost IT professionals and entrepreneurs. A B.Tech in Electronics & Electrical Communication Engineering from the premier Indian Institute of Technology (IIT) at Kharagpur, Arjun established the Prof. G.S. Sanyal School of Tele-communications at his alma mater through a personal endowment. Arjun has also undergone the Advanced Management Program at Harvard Business School. Arjun has been honoured with the coveted Albert Einstein Technology Medal for 2001 by the Jerusalem Fund of Aish HaTorah. As founding member of SPIC-MACAY, Arjun has actively fostered the spread of Indian classical music in schools and colleges in India. Today, SPIC-MACAY is India's largest non-government, not for profit, social and cultural organisation.

The Fashion Guru

— By Ashish Soni

My father is a graduate from IIT Kharagpur and my mother is a PhD in Hindi. I also have a little sister Smita. Ours was what you would call a typical middle class family and I was probably destined for a normal routine life.

I grew up in Zambia and did my secondary education there. With my mom and sister, I moved back to India and completed my senior secondary education from British School in New Delhi.

After school, when my dad was at home for the holidays, he showed me an advertisement in a newspaper one day which was for the admission process for NIFT. I did not know anything about that place. However, my dad encouraged me to go and visit the campus. Never to miss out on a chance to see anything new, I went to Hotel Samrat where there was a makeshift campus of NIFT in those days. There were rooms in the shopping arcade which served as the classrooms and we were supposed to do all our practical learning in one of the banquet halls. Something happened to me that day, and I realised that this was my calling. Since my childhood, I had been interested in seeing what clothes Michael Jackson was wearing, or Madonna's latest shoes. I gave the exam and got selected along with 25 candidates, out of more than 7000 applicants. After completing my Bachelor's in Fashion Science in 1991, I interned with Rohit Bal for almost a year.

However, I knew my dream within me. I knew I had to start a label of my own by the name of 'Ashish N Soni'. That is exactly what I did in 1992 and became the first designer in the country to have a solo fashion showing in 1993.

More than 12 years have passed since then and I have achieved a lot, but know there is a long road ahead. Sometimes I wonder how I knew that fashion was my dream. It's like a child learning to do a jigsaw puzzle. The pieces are always all there in front of you. What is important is that you actually put the right piece in the right position. The sooner you do that, the better it is. If there is something you want to do, if you have a dream, then you must follow it. Else it will irk you for life. This dream requires fire. The fire might be genetic or might be from the surroundings. However, most of the time, it is something which you have inside you and only you know about it. It depends on how much leeway you give for this fire to spread; that decides whether you will be able to fulfil your dream or not.

Always remember that whatever the external circumstances might be, your mindset is your own. There will be minutes or hours or days or even weeks when you might feel low. But then you will realise that it's only you who can get yourself back to a positive frame of mind.

Surely luck plays an important part in achieving success. And I will not deny that I have been lucky. Launching my labels in Dubai in 1995, and London in 1996, had a certain amount of good luck associated with them. But then there is something which is bigger than just being plain lucky. It is the art of recognising the luck and grabbing that opportunity. You just cannot expect to sit around and wait to get lucky. You will have to go out there and make the luck tilt in your favour.

Once you have a positive mindset and fight for your luck, set personal standards and goals for yourself. Ensure that every time you get into the battlefield to achieve your goals, you outdo yourself! And believe me, this way you will always achieve your goals.

I was really glad when Ishan approached me to write for the book. We were talking about the problems which one faces in becoming an entrepreneur. When I look back on my journey of entrepreneurship till date, I realise that the problems which were there a decade back, still exist today and will continue to do so in the future also. However, the dimensions of the problem may change with time. Finding a good team is never easy. I have been lucky, as my sister Smita joined me in the same stream and we work together. The problems of capital and infrastructure are always given constants. As the business grows, the magnitude just becomes bigger. So never think despondently that you are going to face problems when you decide to start your own venture, because it is these very problems which make entrepreneurship so exciting and so dynamic.

Whenever you feel you need help, just go ahead and ask someone for it. There are enough people in the world and someone will surely be ready to help you out. Always have mentors, because they will really guide you to achieve better results. I could not have got where I am today without mine, the greatest of them being my father.

As I end this, I want to leave you with two facts of life I really believe in. The first one is to always differentiate between ambition and greed. This will help you work ethically and be successful in your own eyes. Second, never look back and regret your mistakes. Just learn from them and keep moving forward!

Ashish Soni is a leading fashion designer of India. His label, ASHISH N SONI *retails successfully in select outlets in Bangalore, Kolkata, Hyderabad and Chennai as well as in Dubai, through the largest couture store in the Middle East, Fasateen, and at Selfridges in London and Manchester, UK. He is a regular participant in international fashion shows in cities like New York, London, etc.*

Dance from the Heart

— By Ashley Lobo

I basically belong to Mumbai. I did my schooling at St. Mary's High School, Mount Abu, Rajasthan (a residential school). I later graduated in economics from St. Xavier's College, Mumbai. My father is a retired army officer and my mother is a voice-dynamics trainer. She is also a well-known opera singer and theatre director in Mumbai. I have two sisters: the older one lives in the US and is also an opera singer by profession, while the younger is a businesswoman in Australia.

There is a saying that "you never choose dance, dance chooses you". And that is exactly what happened with me. It was during the '80s. I was back home in Mumbai after having finished Year 10 in boarding school. At that time, my mother was directing a musical production, which was being choreographed by Salome Roy Kapur. Salome was looking for dancers and since I was relatively free and waiting to start Year 11, my mother suggested I audition. I auditioned and...*surprise*!! I was selected—and that's where it all began!

During one of our performances, noted choreographer Karla Singh happened to visit. She was in the middle of casting dancers for another musical production and asked me if I would be interested in working with her. I did. Thereafter, I continued dancing, going from one musical production to another.

Dance in the '80s was not a feasible career choice. At the end of each show, we got Rs.100, which was usually spent the same evening! A lot of fun and good times – but no money! A time came when I had to get serious about a career, and so I joined a company as a management trainee. Over the next two years, I worked hard and got myself to a managerial position, all the while keeping in touch with my dance and theatre. But as I tried to climb the corporate ladder, my dance was increasingly becoming a distraction. And so when my company offered me a transfer/promotion to the New Delhi office, I readily accepted as I thought this would help me focus and take me away from the "distraction" of dance forever.

My life in Delhi was all work, till one day a colleague, who was aware of my dance/theatre background, asked me if I'd be interested in going to audition for a musical. I went to audition as a dancer, and ended up being the choreographer! That musical was "West Side Story", directed by George Pulinkala. It was very well-received and I got rave reviews from all the leading newspapers for my choreographic work. All that attention was very heady for a young 21-year old. I impulsively decided to drop my corporate career and go overseas to study dance. So, here I was, back to dance, this time as a career! It was almost like, no matter how far I tried to run away and follow a more practical career choice, circumstances kept throwing me back into dance. And why did I choose to go overseas, to Australia? Well firstly, there were no formal dance institutes that taught international dance forms in India, and secondly, choosing to have a career in international dance at that time in India was unrealistic and impractical as there was no market for it.

I went on to study dance for five years in Sydney, Australia at the Bodenweiser Dance Centre and at the Sydney Dance

Company and also performed there professionally during that time.

I returned to India for a short holiday in 1994. By then, cable TV had come to India in a big way and because of the exposure to the international art/dance/media, people's awareness of international dance had increased. What I witnessed was a totally different situation to what I had left. One thing, however, hadn't changed – there was still no institution that taught the various international dance forms in their original formats. Moreover, there was no place that taught one how to use the body. Most places just taught steps – great if all you wanted was to be a chorus dancer, but not so great if you wanted to be a soloist or a choreographer.

Therein was born the seed of an idea, a dream that is today *The Danceworx Performing Arts Academy*. And to realise that dream, I finally returned to India in 1998.

Today, I would want to facilitate in some way the creation of dancers who can go on the international stage and match dancers there, in their language, step for step and technique for technique. Furthermore, I dream of something like a dance university: a platform where professors and experts on dance movement from all over the world, of both eastern and western styles, can come together to freely exchange ideas and experiences. I believe this fusion of ideas will create dancers and thinkers from within the country that will be open-minded and forward thinking and will create a universal language of dance that will better global understanding. I believe these young artists, once they take over the reins, will drive the vision of dance to a new level, taking dance forward.

What I have come to believe in my life is that the brain can sometimes confuse us. We are very susceptible to programming, which is stored in the brain. This programming is an ongoing process. The brain is trained and programmed to think practically all the time. Everything has to be logical. Most positives come from the heart, be it passion, joy, strength, happiness and even true pain, while most negatives come from the brain, be it fear or doubt. Vision and belief, on the other hand, are intuitive and come from an inner voice. I believe the trick to life is ignoring the negatives of the brain and listening to and believing in this inner voice. A vision can be organised and executed by the brain, and that is where the practicality of the brain should be used.

I believe that when one wants to build an organisation, one must remember that an organisation is not created by just practical analysis. It is vision and direction. It's always a team effort. What is required is good leadership. One requires leaders who listen to their inner voices, are intuitive, and have a happy, strategic marriage of heart and head. Leaders who have learnt to let neither the brain nor the heart rule in isolation. Leaders whose vision comes from their imagination. Dreamers driven by the heart. Leaders with the courage to try. And who use the brain only for its analytical and logical ability at the correct times, i.e., for organisation and execution only.

One important element I have learnt is that one really needs to love people. One needs to understand what they want and provide them with something they will cherish. One needs to understand and accept that there are different types of people. Having said that, one's ability to align and dialogue with people through marketing then becomes almost imperative. This requires generosity and openness to people and learning. Something I learnt the hard way.

Ishan asked me what it would take to displace me from my position in the international dance scene in India! I must admit it was an unusual question. My answer was that there are too few of us, and that the question of displacement of me (or anyone else for that matter) would never arise. The way the industry is poised today, any new additions will be more than welcome. Today, the industry is looking for more leaders and so new additions will contribute rather than provide competition. Please bring them on – we need them! It'll only widen the market and help us move faster and realise my dream.

Ashley Lobo started The Danceworx Performing Arts Academy in November of 1998 to teach dance along the lines of dance institutes overseas. Currently, its curriculum consists of styles such as Jazz, Classical Ballet, Contemporary Dance and Social Dance styles. Since its inception, the Academy has expanded from a modest base of 100-odd students and 1 studio to a base of over 2500 students and 9 studios. Here, students are challenged to compete with themselves and to break barriers within their own minds to come to a new position of information. The aim of The Danceworx Performing Arts Academy is to help in developing the students' creative potential to the highest possible level and to train and channelise their talent under the able guidance of well-trained teachers in an atmosphere of fun, love and values.

Challenges for the Entrepreneur

— By Dilip Cherian

The challenges of entrepreneurship, of course, come in different configurations, dictated as much by our existential conditions as by the regulatory set-ups and the cultural milieu that we live in. Given the unique conditions prevailing in different societies, it's important to appreciate them as they face the entrepreneurs. While some socio-economic-regulatory conditions help entrepreneurship to bloom, there are others which hinder its growth.

Notwithstanding the importance of the impact of the environment on entrepreneurship, a big part of the entrepreneurial drive is actually anchored on individual qualities of risk-taking ability, passion, perseverance, and 'fire in the belly' to challenge the 'rules of the game'. They truly constitute the essence of entrepreneurship. History bears testimony that great entrepreneurship stories are less written on successful inculcation of training modules and more on a unique constellation of these traits in the individual.

It is often debated, rather passionately, whether entrepreneurship can, like any other stream of knowledge, be taught. The answer surely is not an easy one. For, while the core qualities of an entrepreneur will always remain an embellishment unique to the individual, motivating human mind and channellising energy towards pursuance of independent economic goals are surely amenable to structured training. This enables the participants to appreciate the challenge much better and prepare them to take the entrepreneurial grind with equanimity.

Every generation gives birth to its own genre of successful entrepreneurs. If the Tatas, Birlas, Ambanis, Singhanias and Thapars were the leading lights of the old economy, the Narayana Murthys and Azim Premjis will remain etched in public memory in times to come for having scripted the most thrilling accounts of new economy successes.

Budding entrepreneurs are better served in their endeavours with some prior knowledge about the inherent challenges. This is where the key role of books on the possible problems and prospects facing entrepreneurs in a particular market come in. Write-ups on success stories, too, prove to be a source of inspiration for upcoming entrepreneurs.

A Founder-partner of Perfect Relations, Dilip Cherian is widely regarded as India's 'image guru'. Dilip is also a columnist and a business analyst. Today, he has devoted readers in the Asian Age, the Indian Express and several language newspapers in various parts of the country. He is also a former editor of 'Business India' (India's largest business magazine) and the 'Observer' newspaper. Dilip's outside interests includes work in the social sector. Currently he is a member of the Board of Governors in Advertising Standard Council of India and on the Governing Council of the National Institute of Design. Dilip lives in Delhi with his wife and two children.

Obsessive Passion

— By Dilip Chhabria

The DC Design story is one of obsessive passion. Having completed the Transportation Design course from Art Centre, Pasadena, USA, joining General Motors felt like a statistic in a bureaucratic organisation. I particularly wanted to ensure that hard work could only be motivated by the fact that the benefits should accrue to me rather than to GM, therefore, I left GM within a year.

Obsessive Passion: Passion is gradable. You can have 90-95% or 100%. A 100% passion will decide your continuous enthusiasm for the subject without any distraction. For example, if you are passionate about cars and bikes, this will not do. You need to be extremely focussed on either cars or bikes. You eat, drink, and sleep your subject.

Courage: If your passion is for a subject out of the ordinary, you must possess dollops of courage to take up your career head-on. For example, though I was chided by my parents for drawing in my early youth, I persevered, and had to summon up courage to start DC Design against the wishes of my parents or my wife. My argument at that time was that, even if I fail, we will not go hungry, for we had a roof over our head at the very least. You must never allow yourself choices, for with choices, you will never have a life or death situation, you will never do your best. Consequently, you may fail to deliver that punch, for you can always walk away.

Vision: Most youth do not think in the medium to long-term and often are possessed with the plans of the immediate. It is a rule in life that to be successful you have to build an enduring organisation which is best achieved through an organic and step-by-step approach over the long term. One has to develop the ability to presage future trends and pre-ordain the competitive pressures.

Hard Work: There is no substitute for hard work, and it is often said luck favours when opportunity meets preparedness. The mindset of a successful entrepreneur should be one of not only protecting one's turf but wanting to eat someone else's lunch as well, and that you can only do when you put in real hard work.

Want To Leave A Mark As A Man: All actions and decisions should be based on the fact that you want to endear yourself to people and feel loved and encouraged. This craving makes you a humbler human being capable of better communication, and therefore more effective to get through *his* way.

Making USP: Remember, you have to think of your intrinsic quality and USP of your business. Unless you have a very strong USP, you will not be able to consolidate your business. Also, most youth must remember to build strong brands to ensure that the benefits accrue to the bottom line.

The challenges and hardships are plenty. At the outset, our society is largely risk-averse, and this makes it difficult to do unique things. Businessmen, therefore, must have patience, strong commitment to get over things. Banish anger, and impatience from your mindset. At the end of the day, the fact that you are responsible for providing many a job does make you happy and additionally, letters and calls of appreciation, and to be emulated as a role model spurs me on to a greater challenge and glory.

Dilip Chhabria, Promoter of Dilip Chhabria Design Private Limited, is currently recognised as the leading Automobile Designer in India. Qualified in Transportation Design from Art Centre of Design, Pasadena, USA and worked with General Motors, USA, in the Design Centre. He started his own auto accessory business and became one of the largest auto accessory manufacturers in the country. Using design as a differentiator, Dilip Chhabria has made true the mantra, 'Good Design is Good Business', by establishing a design-based company in a country where intellect was not paid for, valued or protected. A classic case of entrepreneurship has resulted in translating one man's dream and vision into a 300-strong company.

Gaining A Winning Edge

— By Dr. Kiran Mazumdar-Shaw

"At the onset let me congratulate you for the brave and inspiring endeavour. I wish you the very best on your entrepreneurial adventure and the book all the success".

Building an enterprise is like embarking on a voyage of discovery:

There are no finite goals,

No certain destinations,

The joy of an unknown territory lies in its discovery.

Even today, pioneering entrepreneurs traverse unknown paths that result in significant social and economic changes to nations.

The story of Biocon is one such thrilling journey.

Our goal was clear – to prove to the world that we could build a world-class Biotechnology enterprise in India. We had to demonstrate that we could create advanced scientific laboratories for Indian scientists to pursue cutting edge R&D, to ensure that we could benchmark our quality with the very best in the world and above all, to develop the most competitive and innovative technologies to guarantee us the winning edge.

I have always believed in being a path-breaker and embarking on the road less travelled. We pioneered Biotechnology two decades before others even perceived this opportunity. We were the first company in India to develop enzymes, statins and immuno-suppressants. We are the first Asian company to scale up Human Insulin to a global scale and today, we are the first Indian company to develop antibodies at commercial scale.

We started our journey developing enzymes for the food industry and today we are developing antibodies for cancer. Who knows what the future holds? Today, we are committed to addressing challenges of the future like the rest of the world.

I strongly believe if you have a vision, a plan and the conviction, you should follow it and success will come to you. Biocon is testimony to a vision that a team of like-minded people with the same drive to excel can achieve.

Dr. Kiran Mazumdar-Shaw is the Chairman & Managing Director, Biocon Limited. She is the recipient of several prestigious awards including the 'ET Businesswoman of the Year', 'Best Woman Entrepreneur', 'Model Employer', Ernst & Young's 'Entrepreneur of the Year Award' for Life Sciences & Healthcare, 'Leading Exporter', 'Outstanding Citizen', 'Technology Pioneer', etc. Her most cherished awards are however, the PADMASHRI (1989) and PADMA BHUSHAN (2005) presented to her by the President of India, for her pioneering efforts in Industrial Biotechnology.

Globalising a Legacy

— By Mohit Burman

My early days

I was born as a part of one of the well-known and respected corporate families in India which is a boon in itself, but with the biggest of boon comes the biggest of responsibilities. That is also very true with my being part of a lineage that takes pride in being one of the legendary families of the nation.

I studied in two colleges – namely Babson Graduate School of Business, Massachusetts, for my Master's degree in Business Administration, and Richmond College, London, for my Bachelor in Arts in Business Administration & Economics.

College life in the US and UK were completely different. During my graduate days, I could afford to indulge in extra-curricular activities like theatre, riding and water sports. This did not mean that I neglected my studies; I gave equal attention to academics. I have always been a firm believer in the importance of academics. During my Master's degree, however, I was totally committed to academics as the focus was on gaining professional exposure. The US is cutting-edge in management and technology. Studying in the US gave me a perspective on how things worked globally.

Leadership in the atmosphere

I grew up among the leaders of the business world in India, so continuous learning was in progress. In fact, I must tell you that my upbringing had been very much ruled by the family gatherings where I got a wide exposure to the various happenings round the world, as these family gatherings were more or less a discussion forum on not only the world of the business but also on life as a whole.

There are many factors that contribute to good leadership. And, whether someone is naturally a good leader or not. Anyone can become a good leader provided he gets the right exposure and has the willingness to learn. However, the leadership qualities that are required to make a good leader vary for different people. A great leader has to have passion; drive to achieve; ambition to grow and ability to lead. I strongly believe that the one who is passionate about what he does is the one who is likely to excel in whatever he takes on in life.

Challenges of today

Even today, I face lots of challenges. Dabur India Limited is the fourth largest FMCG company in India with interests in health care, personal care and food products. Today, Dabur has a consolidated turnover of Rs.1537 crore (minus Balsara acquisition) and is an aggressively growing company. The biggest challenge that I face is to ensure that this growth is maintained and accelerated. In fact, being entrepreneurs with greater risk-taking abilities, it is always expected that we identify bigger and faster growth opportunities and accelerate the growth momentum beyond industry average.

We not only need to live up to people's expectations but also our own expectations as we set definite goals for us and see to it that it is achieved over a certain period of time. The competition is within our own self; and as entrepreneurs and as professionals; we are continuously trying to outdo our own performance. That certainly is pressure, and that also is sheer excitement.

Passion and entrepreneurship

Passion is a very subjective trait. For me as a person, life is a beautiful journey steered by passion. I try and live every moment of it to the fullest. Passion for me is excelling in my work and achieving the maximum from every situation and challenge. A drive to excel and succeed in whatever I undertake would define passion for me. It is the same passion I see in the authors of the book. Their drive to promote technology among students is a much-needed element in completing professional technical education today.

I have always viewed entrepreneurship as an activity having no set rules and it does involve a lot of risk. It's an art that can only be mastered once you become a part of the business. Many people have commented widely on how to become a successful 'entrepreneur', the word sounds really jazzy and corporate but when it comes to be a player in the real arena, it's then that the real fun begins.

It is all about identifying opportunities and taking risks: You risk failure, you risk your sanity, you risk losing the support of loved ones who don't understand why you're devoting 18 hours a day to something that may or may not fly, to name a few. But if you take the time to research each decision you make along the way, most likely, you'll succeed.

Going after what you want is good, as long as you work hard to get it. So take risks, yes, but take them wisely. Then you won't have any trouble saying, "I got it" on a regular basis. I strongly believe that one should also aim higher than the goal you have set for yourself; it helps you in achieving more from life.

Go, follow your dreams

All the young entrepreneurs who have promised themselves to follow their dreams, remember: think big and dream bigger. Dreams are the stepping-stones to success. Someone has rightly said, "One should always aim for the moon, even if the arrow lands in stars you would have reached higher." Dreams can turn into reality in today's environment. Many companies and entrepreneurs have made it to the top slot in the last few years. Second, success knows no short cuts. A vibrant and strong entrepreneurial culture seems to be emerging in India. As the younger lot is exposed towards international best practices, entrepreneurship is likely to emerge as a source of competitive advantage for the country. I believe that the seeds of entrepreneurship, i.e., less government interference and its increased role as a facilitator, fewer bureaucratic hurdles and easy access to capital are being sown already. I would strongly advise all the budding entrepreneurs to have a strong foundation created by education and knowledge.

Mr. Mohit Burman is a Director on the Board of Balsara Home, Balsara Hygiene and Besta Cosmetics, companies acquired and now subsidiaries of Dabur India.

Escorts Towards Newer Horizons

— By Nikhil Nanda

The manufacturing activities of Escorts Group comprise Tractors, Construction Equipment and Auto Components. As the Chief Operating Officer of Escorts Group, it is my responsibility of steering ahead these three major business operations. The CEOs of these manufacturing operations work directly under my stewardship. Having set an aim for myself to accomplish a momentous position with a substantial market share for the said business, I also aspire to judiciously reduce gratuitous cost and instil dynamism in the group hierarchy. It goes without saying that all what I aim at and aspire for is taxing and warrants immense amount of toil, but then, there is no proxy for hard work. The target that I have set for myself necessitates that I am more proactive with more involvement in inter-departmental and intra-departmental proceedings.

Though I was born with a silver spoon in my mouth, I have done my share of slumming. No extra provisions were bestowed upon me. Local buses were mode of conveyance for me, too. This carried on to Doon School, the place where I spent meaningful formative years of my life. Again, there was no different yardstick to measure my capabilities and performance. This is where the value of discipline moulded my mind. On merit alone, I secured a place for myself at Wharton when my parents could have easily supported me.

The boundless energy of youth keeps propelling me to take Escorts to a glorious summit where I yearn it to be, and there is no time to squander. When I was 12, my grandfather, (Late) Mr. HP Nanda taught me that I needed to be passionate about my work to achieve success. My maternal grandfather, (Late) Mr. Raj Kapoor often used to tell me to look into the mirror and tell myself that I can do it – and half the battle is won. Self-work has been a part of my upbringing and it is an integral part of my personality. I nurture this fiery passion within me to take Escorts to newer heights and every living moment I strive to let this show. My family environment, my education and the able guidance have tutored the sense of immense responsibility that lies on me in carrying ahead the glorious legacy of Escorts. I will always be true to myself and to my company in carrying out my responsibilities and fulfilling the cherished dreams.

Introspection and critical self-assessment would always shed light on our weaknesses and flaws or any other gaffe that we might have committed inadvertently or otherwise. This will surely make all of us better entrepreneurs. This would also augment our understanding and control of our respective business ventures. Sincere and unremitting efforts along with clear vision to achieve pre-determined goals have to be the locus and focus of our business activities. It's important to fix targets for oneself and then self-strive to achieve them too.

It is the deep-set yearning and hunger to stride ahead and achieve the set objectives that gets transformed into passion for work. The relentless drive within manifests in self-belief. This very energy and passion are the resources that bridge the gap between where you are today and where you want to be tomorrow.

Challenges are an integral part of life. Today, I face the daunting task and the challenge to motivate my team while continuously exhibiting leadership to them. The vision and objectives must be shared with the team. Effective leadership must also generate positive energy and passion to keep the team brimming with enduring energy and spirit.

Nikhil Nanda is the Executive Director and Chief Operating Officer of Escorts Group. He has the overall responsibility for managing the Group's Agri, Construction and Engineering businesses. Together with business heads, he is leading the corporation's campaign to transform its culture towards efficiency and aggressive growth. Born in March 1974, Mr. Nikhil Nanda is an alumnus of Wharton Business School, Philadelphia, USA. Having graduated in Business Administration in 1995, he majored in Management and Marketing, before undergoing professional training with JC Bamford Excavators Ltd., UK.

Entrepreneurs and Entrepreneurship

— By Prof. Patrick Turner

There have been many attempts to shed light on what makes somebody want to become an entrepreneur, and there is still a widespread idea that entrepreneurs are, by and large, people who drop out of school when they are in their teens, go and invent something in the shed at the bottom of the garden, start a company, and go on to fame and fortune. Clearly, entrepreneurs with this profile do exist, but despite popular entrepreneur folklore, they are very much in the minority.

In fact, the only recipe that stands up to critical examination is that you are more likely to become an entrepreneur if someone in your environment is or has been one, your father for instance, or some other family member.

However, your environment includes more than just your family, and so it can also be said that if there is a strong entrepreneurial community where you are brought up – your hometown, or even a cluster of towns in your area – then this can also encourage you to think of becoming an entrepreneur yourself. It's not just a question of icons, or role models; it's more a matter of entrepreneurship appearing to you, in those you see around you, as a perfectly normal and widely practiced way of pursuing a career.

This perception of entrepreneurship as a 'normal' career option can be helped enormously by the teaching of entrepreneurship. Since I have been a professor of entrepreneurship at the international business school, INSEAD, I have often been asked if it is possible to teach entrepreneurship. The answer is, of course, the principles of entrepreneurship can be taught. If they could not, that would make entrepreneurship the one and only human activity impossible to teach, which is an absurdity. In fact, entrepreneurship education can help people to understand how to go about validating an idea to determine whether it is a viable commercial opportunity, how to go about planning and launching a new company with all that this entails, and then how to run it, including the pitfalls and danger areas and how to avoid them.

But it can do much more than this. It can positively influence an individual's perception of the risks entailed in becoming an entrepreneur so that he realises that the risks he/she perceives can be managed in such a way as to radically reduce them. This, on its own, is enough to make many people consider becoming an entrepreneur, whereas before they would have been afraid to do so.

There is, in fact, empirical evidence of this, which demonstrates that education and training in entrepreneurship can help entrepreneurs increase their firm's chance of survival, and to a lesser extent, it can help make the resulting business more profitable.

For instance, it is important to know, as all entrepreneurs do, that the first stages of a new venture launch are often somewhat akin to white-water canoeing. You launch your carefully crafted business plan out on to the waters of reality like a kayak, and before you know it all hell has broken loose. Rocks (e.g., slower than anticipated sales growth) and boulders (e.g., longer than anticipated product development costs and lead times) emerge with frightening suddenness out of the spray, and all your energies and waking hours are devoted to keeping your fragile craft from getting smashed to pieces on them by the raging current that is remorselessly carrying you along.

Then, if you navigate the rapids successfully, you reach a calmer period. The brute fight for survival is behind you and you no longer have sleepless nights wondering how you are going to pay salaries this month. True, the river still holds dangers, but you are past the initial life-threatening stretch.

You are now faced with a choice: either you opt to hold your business at the level it has reached, or you decide to go for growth. If you decide on the latter course of action, then you will find yourself faced with a new collection of issues you didn't even suspect existed when you were first trying to get your venture launched. As your company grows, the factors that were less important, or quite simply not even considered at the very beginning, progressively assume a much greater importance, while at the same time, your ability to act unilaterally in "shoot from the hip" mode is steadily reduced.

During all this time, you will have experienced the roller-coaster ride of an entrepreneur, and if you have some knowledge beforehand of what to expect, then your chances of survival will be greatly increased.

Here are some words of advice from some past INSEAD students who have become entrepreneurs:

- You need the ambition to create wealth by investing in yourself, adding value to the companies you run, and approaching challenges where the risk is calculated, measured and controlled. Analyse situations quickly and use the results to make informed decisions that lead to action. And since you'll never be totally prepared or ready, just do it! *(Timothy Bovard – American)*
- Make sure your idea is market-proven and then just do it, one step at a time. You may want to run a global company and hire a CEO immediately, but remember that you have to start at the beginning. The best piece of advice I can give though, is to show no fear. *(Hans Hammer – German)*

- It's important for an entrepreneur to understand his or her business well. First, develop expertise in the business area in which you want to specialise. Second, build networks and contacts that will help you in your business. Start building a capital base to take risks, so that you are not dependent on your business income for survival. This will help you focus on the task ahead instead of worrying about your next month's expenses. *(Krishnan Varadarajan – Indian)*
- Double check the uniqueness of your idea, your knowledge of the industry, and above all, your commitment to dedicate long hours and weekends to your business for little or no pay for the next three to five years. Do not underestimate the complexity of the tasks that will be required of you. Assemble a team you totally believe in and get as many senior contacts in the industry of your choice as possible in order to get a headstart. Get the financing sorted at an early stage, as time will be at a premium. The last thing you want is to have to worry about money. *(Danielle de Winter – British)*
- There's a lot of selling involved – convincing investors to put up money, and getting the first customers on board. You need lots of energy to get things going, along with good organisation skills. You need to be resourceful all the time and keep adapting to make things grow. *(Michael Doherty – British)*

Being an entrepreneur is probably the most thrilling and fulfilling professional experience you can have. But beware. It also makes you unemployable. For, once this entrepreneurship thing has got into your blood, you've got it for life. You're hooked. And it's by no means an easy road and it's not for everybody. For although the highs are more euphoric than any other business experience you are ever likely to have, the lows can be very stressful.

As it was graphically put by Jeffrey Timmons in his book *New Venture Creation*, entrepreneurship is a combination of "experiencing the deep, dark canyons of uncertainty and ambiguity, and walking the breathtaking highlands of success".

Patrick Turner is an Affiliate Professor of Entrepreneurship at INSEAD. After a business career, including running his own companies, Professor Turner joined INSEAD in 1999, teaching MBA courses on acquisitions, new business creation, and managing growth. He has since taught in France, Spain and South America. He is the co-author of a book on entrepreneurship in Asia, published in 2005, and is currently working on another book on entrepreneurship to be published later on this year.

Yes, You Can Do It!

— By Pradeep Chopra

We are like you but we took the decision.

Let me first introduce myself: My name is Pradeep Chopra. I am a Punjabi, born and brought up in Delhi. I am married and live with my wife and parents in Delhi. I belong to a typical, Indian middle-class family and my parents are government servants.

I did my schooling from Central School and after a lot of hard work, got into IIT in the year 1995. I was a studious guy at IIT and was considered an ordinary guy. Although I dreamed, I didn't belong to those guys who were highly active in various extra-curricular activities at IIT.

After I graduated in 1999, I joined TCS (Tata Consultancy Services) as a software engineer. I started my career in Mumbai and had great fun in my first job. I fully enjoyed my stay at TCS and Mumbai for 16 months before I decided to move close to my batch mates in the US.

While working in TCS, I got a highly paid (in dollars) job in one of the big five consulting companies. It was July of 2000 and I had to join this new job in the US in October, when I was to get my visa. So, I resigned from TCS and came to Delhi (my home) in September, thinking of joining my new job in October-November.

After I reached here, I got in touch with two of my batch mates (Kapil Nakra and Purvesh Sharma) from IIT. They were working together and one fine day (on October 14, 2000), they decided to open their own company and asked me if I would join them. It was a very surprising and difficult question for me. But, without taking much time I said "Yes". Howsoever difficult the decision was, it was the beginning of a new life for all of us.

The only decision we took was that we would do something of our own. Beyond that, we had no clue of what we would do, where we would get funds, etc. The only thing we were clear about was that we had a great team between the three of us. Combining all our savings, we had Rs.70,000 to start with.

It is exciting, adventurous and lots of fun!

We had a big dream and we were excited to jump onto the entrepreneurial bandwagon. Also, we were highly optimistic and I must say we were equally unrealistic to begin with. When we started, it was the peak of the dotcom bubble. So our beginning coincided with the bust of the dotcom era.

In the very beginning, with the bust of this bubble, we confronted the reality. Although it was shocking, I must say it was very valuable for us. It taught us many lessons which became the foundation for our success. We might have otherwise been ruined by the ramifications of the dotcom bust.

Since we had no 'business idea', we thought we'd start with doing a few projects, and assumed that money will flow in from the beginning itself, and easily. With a great amount of hard work, we got a couple of projects but didn't make more than a few thousand rupees. Some of the guys who gave us work ditched us, and we did not get paid for those efforts.

Being from a middle-class family, we had to face a lot of pressure from our families. Naturally, we (particularly I) didn't fit into their expectations due to which there was resistance from my family. We used to work day and night in the beginning and we were not earning anything. For them, we were working too hard without getting any returns. In this context, let me share something very funny with you.

To hide my hard work (with no returns) from my parents and to pretend to them that it wasn't only hard work, I used to switch to 'playing games on my PC screen', when my parents came to my room and looked at my PC.

Equally painful was the peer pressure. Most of our batch mates were living a cushy life in the US with lots of dollars in their pockets and bank accounts.

I still remember that for some months I used to have not more than Rs.10 in my pocket to spend for the whole day. We could not even afford to watch movies for some time. Nevertheless, we had great fun, enjoyed each movement and were clear that we would soon meet success.

Learnt the hard way and still learning...

Throughout the journey, we learnt many lessons and we've been learning something new every day. Some of these lessons we learnt the hard way, and these are the lessons we can't forget for our lifetime. Let me share some of our learnings:

1. Plans are Useless and Planning is Priceless

In the beginning, our focus used to be on making the 'good plan'. We were more concerned about 'whether the plan looks good or not' than 'is this a realistic plan or are we ready to bet on it?' In the initial phases, we participated in many business plan competitions. In the first competition, we were not even short-listed. In the second one, we reached the finals and in the 3rd competition (Eureka, IIT Mumbai), we were the winners. The difference in our approach was that we shifted from making the 'good plan' to 'realistic', and the plan we ourselves were ready to 'bet on'.

Over the years, we spent huge amounts of time in making different levels of plans and one of the great lessons we learnt is 'Plans are useless and Planning is Priceless'. It basically says that the plan you create may have to be thrown away in the end but the process through which you make the plan will always be valuable and remain with you.

2. Quality is Paramount

After the sale of our first product, we were very excited to grow. In order to grow fast, we decided to launch many products. In this rush for growth, we forgot that 'we can't compromise on the quality' to achieve the desired goals. So, in a very short span of time, we launched a lot of new products with decreasing quality.

Later on, the inferior quality products backfired and stopped our growth. In this process, we realised that 'quality is paramount'. It's better to do less (whether it's a product or service) and of superior quality than to do a lot, but of inferior or even average quality.

3. Being close to customer is the key to success in any business

We made the first product by chance; on a recommendation by a friend. After developing the first product, we had many questions to answer. For example:

i) What should be the price?

ii) What should be our next product?

To answer these questions, our approach used to be to have a discussion among ourselves, do some search on Google and take a decision. And, we didn't have success after the 1st product. After a long time, we realised that we were missing one of the critical and essential business elements – it was 'having our customer or potential customer to be part of our discussion'. Today, it makes a huge difference in the chances of our success of any such decision.

Let me give you an example to communicate the importance of 'knowing your customer'. You have a shop at Janpath and you sell shirts. The best price at which you can sell the shirts is Rs 75. A very ordinary-looking customer comes to your shop and asks for the price of a shirt. In order to sell the shirt, you say its price is Rs 150. This person bargains with you and finally pays you Rs 100. But the truth is that this customer was ready to pay Rs 150 for the same shirt. If you knew it, you could have asked for Rs 200 and he surely would have paid you Rs 150. Thus, had you known your customer, you could have made 50% more revenue. The reverse is also true; you may be the customer and you may know the best price of the seller.

4. Financial control

This is one lesson we learnt very hard. All of us are engineers and none of us have any formal education in finance. Finance was one area which none of us were interested in. Thanks to our advisor, we learnt the essentials of financial control after four years, at a time when we were in deep losses. The surprising part is that in our minds we were sure that we are in profit but actually we were in deep losses. On realising the truth, we had to let go of more than 25% of people at Whizlabs.

Today, we are clear that whether we like it or not, financial visibility is the most critical aspect of any business. Realising it and controlling it, we got profitable once again after a period of a year of losses.

Success had to come

In spite of all the ups and downs, profits and losses, we were clear that success was going to be the by-product of our passion and hard work. Success is not measured by amount of revenues and profits. You may decide to close your venture but it doesn't mean you've failed. It only means closure of your business and you can yet be successful as an entrepreneur, provided you learn the lessons offered by your decision and move forward to the next game.

I know of a friend who is a very successful entrepreneur today and he had to shut his first *three* ventures. Had he taken those closures as failure, the success he has today would not have been possible.

The Future is Bright

Today, we are very clear that our future is bright, whether our current business grows to the desired levels or not. The respect we get today from our peers, seniors, juniors, family members, fellow entrepreneurs, and successful business people is awesome. I really feel proud about the decision we took five years back.

Our success is primarily based on a few critical factors:

1. Team is everything – I never before understood the importance of the team the way I realised it while being an entrepreneur. I am clear what they mean when venture capitalists say that they really bet on the team and not the idea. Idea is merely 5-10% of the whole game. Like 'employees leave their boss, not the organisation', so do 'people invest on people and not the idea'.
2. Openness – One of the strengths we have is that we had always been open to acknowledge our own mistakes and willing to learn from others, specially the people who've travelled the path we are travelling today. This is the reason why one of our advisors decided to join us.

   Here, I would like to share an example I read recently from the book *Mastery*, by George Leonard. This example is actually taken from the book *Zen Mind, Beginner's Mind* and discussed in *Mastery*. In this, a Zen master talks about slow and fast learners using the example of four kinds of horses: excellent ones, good ones, bad ones, and poor ones. The excellent horse will run left and right, slow and fast, at the driver's will, *before* it sees the shadow of the whip. The good one will run as well as the first one, just before the whip reaches its skin. The bad one will run when it feels pain on its body, while the poor one will run only after the pain penetrates to the marrow of its bones. You can imagine how difficult it is for the poor one to learn to run.

3. Care for people – From the beginning, we were clear that we are up to creating value for everyone associated with us, and for the country. So, we've always been concerned about each and every person 'working with us' (we don't want people to 'work *for* us' but to 'work *with* us'), and everyone 'serves' (our customers).

The REAL Factor – 'We took the decision'

Yes, I really mean it! The REAL reason behind our success (or anyone else's who has been an entrepreneur) is the decision they took to jump into the game. Since I started my first job, I've seen a lot of people waiting for the 'right day' to come when they would start their own company. But, the 'right day' never comes. The day you take the decision is the right day. So, the question is: 'when do you want the right day for you?".

Pradeep Chopra is Co-founder and Head, Sales, at Whizlabs. A graduate from IIT Delhi, Pradeep has strong understanding of IT education domain. His strengths are Innovation and Communication. His responsibilities include strategic alliances, partnerships and the development of new markets for Whizlabs. Whizlabs has helped over 400,000 people in getting certified and advancing their careers at a whopping success rate of 99.7%. The best practices and standards like ISO 9001:2000 have been implemented to achieve this high rate of success and unmatched quality.

Spreading the Technology Information

— By Pradeep Gupta

I joined HCL way back in 1977, after completing my engineering at IIT Delhi in 1975 and my MBA at IIM Calcutta. HCL had just started, and the atmosphere was highly entrepreneurial. We were the first MBA recruits in HCL.

After three years at HCL, I branched out on my own and, with the help of a few associates, started a small infotech company, which commenced with data processing, software development, and training. These were early days for the Information Technology industry. Even today's ubiquitous PC was not out yet. Then, in the early '80s, came the PC, and in certain ways, the boom was as big as the dotcom boom of the late '90s – bringing with it great opportunities for entrepreneurs. Therefore, in 1982, I set up CyberMedia.

According to me, for any venture, there are four important ingredients – which also happen to be the *mantras* behind CyberMedia's success:

- Inspiration
- Aspiration
- Perspiration, and
- Respiration

According to me, **Inspiration** can come anywhere. The idea for CyberMedia came in a cozy Defence Colony barsati – our *adda*, as the Bengalis would say! Two of my friends talked about bringing out a newsletter – *Livestock Times* – animatedly planning it, talking about it. For me, that was an eye-opener. My Inspiration! I felt the need to bring out a newsletter for the Information Technology industry, which brings me to my next ingredient – Aspiration.

Aspiration I define as the passion and belief of an entrepreneur. To soar, you need will, wings, and wind. There has to be hunger in the belly to succeed. The product, when we finally came out with it, was not a newsletter; it was a magazine – ***Dataquest***. But, while the planning was going on, there were a large number of critics who thought that a publication dedicated to IT would never succeed. Even prior to the launch of the venture, two critical people – my editor and the production guy – had to leave due to personal reasons. There was a period of apprehension. I didn't know anything of publishing, so how was I going to build a team? But I was so passionate about the concept that more people joined me and we formed what goes by the name of CyberMedia Limited today. So, when you aspire you face risks, it's your passion and your belief that stands by you.

When Rajat asked me my views on how to get people in a start-up company, I said it's again the passion and the belief. You have to play all the roles – from the peon to the MD – and take decisions at all levels because you are responsible for the motivation of your team. And that is what I mean by **Perspiration** – the sheer hard work, the sweat and the grind. As they say, "No pain, no gain." An entrepreneur has to put in long hours; take numerous decisions beyond his area of expertise; live with uncertainty, and play multiple roles. Above role, there is also the risk. But, it all depends on how you look at it. It's either "Nothing ventured, nothing lost" or "Nothing ventured, nothing *gained.*"

Of course, a very important part of business is Respiration – my fourth ingredient. A majority of businesses in India fail to flourish or remain small because of this factor. By **Respiration**

I mean to be able to let go, to make space, to breathe. For that, you need to overcome some common problems.

- **The passion reduces** – Entrepreneurs often become comfortable with what they have achieved and want to remain in that comfort zone. But if you stand still, you would be left behind by those who are running.
- **Inability to delegate** – I'll explain this with an example. A child grows well when he/she is separated from his/her mother – weaning – considered very important for a child's development and growth. In your case, the business is the child and you are the mother – both need to separate out a bit. This essentially means that you need to share decision-making and, ultimately, certain decisions should never require your call. Many businesses fail to grow when the business owner wants to take all the decisions. Limited time means limited decisions, leading to limited growth.
- **Partnership related problems** – A major cause for business failure. All the partners in the business have their own thought-process and hence, react to different situations in their own different ways. This makes clear distinction of work between different partners very important, so you don't tread on each other's toes.
- **Resources** – You need to have your cash cows, and your first priority should be to generate these cash cows. Because for growth, it is necessary to continuously look at more resources.

Ishan asked me my views on a very important aspect of business – Competition. I believe that competition will always be there, even if you are the first movers. The best way to face them is to find your USP. Your USP will drive your business. I'll give another example here. Some time after the launch of *Dataquest*, *India Today* launched a competing magazine,

Computers Today. We had to strategise and think of ways to compete with *India Today*. We sat down, we brainstormed, and we realised that we could not be better than *India Today* in distribution or production. However, we had better domain knowledge. At the same time, being from the IT industry, our relationships with other technology people were excellent. This – our strong industry understanding and our relationships – became our USP. Thus, it is important that you define your USP over your competitor well.

And then you can go on to rule the world!

Pradeep Gupta is a passionate first generation entrepreneur. He is the Managing Director of CyberMedia. He has over 27 years of experience in the IT industry. Well-networked in the IT and media industry in India, he has provided strategic consultancy to the Government of India, to formulate India's software export strategy. Pradeep Gupta is also General Partner of Infinity Venture Fund, and is on the Investment Management Committee of Punjab Ventures. He is Ex-Chairman of eGurucool.com and Secretary of the Association of Indian Magazines; a Board Member, TiE Delhi; and Chair of Pan IIT in India. He is a graduate in Electrical Engineering from IIT Delhi and a PGDBM from IIM Calcutta. He is also the recipient of the Distinguished Alumni Award of IIT Delhi, 2001.

Creating a Groundswell of Computer Professionals

— By Rajendra S. Pawar

Bringing people and computers together

At NIIT, we began with the vision of bringing people and computers together. This beginning was also the initial period of the PC. It was found that as the power of the PC grew and it became feature-rich, the human-computer interface was changing value systems and institutions. Step by step, the PC world was seen as necessarily a distributive world, which gave primacy to the opportunities that information in the hands of each individual in an organisation could give to the whole of it. Networking multiplied the power of each participant in the network not only by the number of participants in it but also by a multiplier of that number. This revelation led to the rapid popularity of the networked world through such devices as Information Superhighways and finally the Internet and the enabling technology of the World Wide Web. I believe NIIT has created a groundswell of thousands of computer professionals through its vast network of education centres. This has become possible through the efforts of our local business partners who, while offering NIIT-benchmarked education, have also become highly successful entrepreneurs. While many multinationals offer investment and employment opportunities, NIIT is unique not only because it is an Indian multinational, but also because its business model ensures development of local entrepreneurs and proliferation of IT skills.

Rural initiative

In 1999, NIIT set up public-private partnerships with state governments and now provides IT education to millions of children in rural India. Tied to that, NIIT scientists are researching the role of technology and informatics in primary education. The idea is to make it possible for children ranging in age from 6 to 14 to learn many things on their own without the need for a teacher. I believe this system of collaborative learning and a self-organising system can be built into a sustainable, for profit business. We adopted a socially relevant entrepreneurship model for NIIT. We provide scholarships to the poorest of the poor and this initiative has helped educate hundreds of thousands of children in developing countries. The goal is to release the natural energy and hunger for education of the kids, release their willingness of collaborating, not fighting against each other.

I am no visionary

As NIIT became bigger by the day, the industry started calling me a visionary. But I hate tags. I would prefer if people say "If that dummy can do it, so can I!" Balance is the key. Balance between everything. What Gautam Buddha called the Middle Path. Any extreme runs the risk of becoming unmanageable.

Teamwork is the key

Teamwork is the key to entrepreneurial success. More importantly, there is the team think. We have very intense, heated discussions. Outsiders at our monthly meetings think this place is going to explode! Then at the tea break, everybody behaves as if nothing happened. The ability to encourage people to express controversial views and then look for meaning in those, is a great strength. You have to see the other point of view. By encouraging criticism, you create a negative feedback loop. A positive feedback loop can send you into a spiral. In designing a stable system, a negative feedback loop is a must.

Leaders should be vulnerable to followers. For example, when you articulate what you propose to do, you are faced with the reality of making it happen. You become accountable, vulnerable.

Leaders must care

As leaders, we will have to make ourselves most vulnerable. We have to define integrity and then stick to it. There is a tremendous looking up to a leader – the leader means something that they (everybody else) want to be. The leader must care. He has to mean something, represent some value while, at the same time, be vulnerable enough to be questioned, fought with and be fun to be with.

Rajendra S. Pawar, Chairman, NIIT, an Indian IT industry leader and visionary, ranks among India's finest entrepreneurs. He helped create and nurture NIIT, Asia's number one IT education company and NIIT Technologies, India's leading IT solutions provider. A respected opinion leader and thinker, Pawar has spearheaded several IT industry initiatives. As Chairman of IT association, MAIT, during its formative years, when the process of economic liberalisation had just begun, Pawar used the platform to give voice to the industry's aspirations and strengthen the organisation. Ernst & Young India named him its first 'Master Entrepreneur of the Year' in 1999. He has also played significant roles in guiding India's national IT efforts. Pawar is a founding member of Nasscom. He holds a B. Tech degree in Electronics from the Indian Institute of Technology, Delhi. He is a member of the International Business Council of the World Economic Forum and member of the IT Governors body. Pawar has also been working closely with India's well-known educational institutions like Indian School of Business and Indira Gandhi National Open University.

Dare to Dream, Dare to Fail, Dare to Resurrect, Dare to Succeed

— By Raveena Raj Kohli

When you follow a dream, chances are you often have to wake up and smell the coffee.

That's really OK.

Because it's going to just make you more alert and focussed in turning that dream into reality.

Never be afraid of a setback. Never lose sight of the future. The means are but stumbling blocks to achieve what will be yours in the end...

If you have dreamt it, it's yours already.

No machine can ever replace the need for human beings. And no enterprise can succeed if it doesn't carry people along with it. And it's always the little people that count the most.

Don't try to fit what feels forced. And listen to your instincts. A dream comes naturally...you can't force yourself to dream it. But once you are awake, it's up to you to realise it.

Raveena Raj Kohli is the former President and CEO, Star News. She also serves as the CEO of HFCL - Nine Broadcasting.

Putting your Money Where your Mouth Is

— By Sandeep Tyagi

First of all, let me congratulate the authors of this book, Ishan Gupta and Rajat Khare, for taking the initiative to put together a book on entrepreneurship. In a country like India, which is stepping onto the world-stage as a new economic powerhouse after decades of languishing on the sidelines, entrepreneurship has a critical role to play. The raw energy unleashed by entrepreneurs brings resources and capabilities to the most deserving areas in the fastest way possible. It is the cutting edge of the capitalistic system.

I have been asked to write a few words about my own entrepreneurial journey.

I am a management consultant by profession but an entrepreneur by calling. I worked for a couple of prestigious consulting firms in New York. My work involved advising large Fortune 100 financial institutions on management issues. The marketing pitch that we used with our clients was that we typically generate twenty times our fees in value for our clients. This always sounded odd to me, because, why would any sane person give away 95% of the value they were creating. So I decided to start my own firm. That was six years ago.

Over the years, I have learnt a lot more about entrepreneurship. In 2001, we decided to build an office in India. While call centre work was being done out of India, there was little sign of high-end work being done from there at that time. It was not clear that the kind of consulting work we do, which is typically high tech and performed onsite, could be done offshore. To add even more uncertainty, we were making the decision right at the time of the 9/11 attacks. In fact, I remember flying out to India on the first flight out of Newark airport post 9/11 attacks, on September 14, 2001. What seemed like a risky decision at that time has proven to be a highly successful venture. Today, over 70% of all our client engagements have team members from our India office.

Everyone has an opportunity to be an entrepreneur. In essence, entrepreneurship is the ability to dream about a better future and risk some part of the current gratification in pursuit of a bigger objective. So go ahead, make your own dream a reality. You ought to give yourself a chance!

Sandeep Tyagi is the Managing Principal and Founder of the consulting and outsourcing firm, Inductis and has led the firm through its rapid growth and success. Since 2000, Inductis has been bringing together strategy and analytics to achieve measurable results for clients. Prior to founding Inductis, he was a partner at the Mitchell Madison Group (MMG), an eminent global strategy consulting firm. Mr. Tyagi has published articles in publications such as the 'Journal of Business Strategy and Directorship'. He is a member of the Young Presidents Organisation (YPO). He is a board member of the Indian Institute of Technology Delhi, Excellence Foundation, a non-profit that supports the development of IIT Delhi into a world-class institution, and a Charter Member of TiE. Mr. Tyagi holds an MBA from Columbia Business School, and a B.Tech in Computer Science from IIT Delhi. He lives in New Jersey with his wife and two children.

Entrepreneurship in the Internet Era

— By Tarun Wig

> *"Don't ask what the world needs. Ask what makes you come alive, and go do it. Because what the world needs is people who have come alive."*
> *— Howard Thurman*

Reading this quote three years ago inspired a nineteen-year old to follow his passion and life-long goal – to be an entrepreneur. Entrepreneurship has to be probably one of the most ambiguous words in the history of the English language. I was first introduced to this word by my family grocer who asked me as a three-year old kid whether I would like to grow up to be an entrepreneur like him. I would be the first one to admit that the word did not have the same hold on me as it does now. Over a period of time, biographies of people like Dhirubhai Ambani, Lee Iacocca, etc., gave this word a completely different perspective for me. I went on to understand that the word simply means maximum utilisation and growth of the three fundamentals of life – time, money and emotion.

These factors are the bread and butter of any entrepreneur. We worship these three fundamentals: on a conscious level for someone who has created a million-dollar business, or on an unconscious level if he is striving to do so.

About three years back, it dawned on me that these three fundamentals were pushing me towards the latest and probably most wonderful boon to technopreneurs – the Internet.

The greatest discovery of my generation is that a human being can alter his life by altering his attitudes of mind.

– William James

The virtual market has changed the way companies perceive themselves. The market is now wider, global and the competition is intense. The Net is a market of extremes. This market does not allow you the comfort of the middle path where you can exist without growth. Today, you continuously strive for excellence and reach the top...or you gradually die down. For instance, Google, the most used search engine, with the largest user database spent $293 million in research and development, general and administrative expenditure in the third quarter, 2005 compared to $157 million spent the previous year.

The first step to utilise this new opportunity is – very simple – accept it. Today, it does not take five years to be a global leader, an accepted and recognised brand the world over; it takes five months or less.

Once you have accepted the Net, the next step is to understand it. Before undertaking the online campaign for AppinLabs HomTech product, each member of the Online Marketing team spent close to 1000 hours alone on researching the various tools and methodologies used.

In every age, successful entrepreneurs have managed to use the existing tools to create a new structure. Innovations based on geography can only yield limited dividends. A world-renowned brand is not a product of some random confluence of events. For instance, we took conscious steps to introduce technological innovations in every implemented process.

The use of latest technology methodologics is necessary not only to reduce cost and effort but also to increase the process of reaching out to the users quickly. In today's world, you have to reach out to your clients through multiple means. The art of *touching the client* to make sure that client loyalty is maintained has never been easier with the various technological breakthroughs present today.

Technology is necessary to map the real market and the virtual market. To explain this concept completely in one article is impossible. A lot more detail and successful case studies are covered in our upcoming book *Business Today – The Age of the Technopreneurs* where we discuss the introduction and use of technology to create a global brand.

We look forward to introduce to you the advent of science and technology in the economic development of the country.

Tarun Wig is the Co-Founder and Director of AppinLabs, Global leaders in promoting Information Security and Ethical Hacking.

Sharp Focus is a Must

— By Vishnu R. Dusad

I will begin this with a story. When you have to burn a piece of paper with sunlight, how do you do it? You bring a lens and focus the sun's rays at one point. What happens when you move the lens's position again and again? The paper doesn't burn. But when you keep the lens static and all sun rays focussing at one point, you will see the paper burning. The same is the case with an entrepreneur's focus. When he focusses, he produces tremendous results. A very sharp focus initially is a must in entrepreneurship. The greater the focus, the greater is the success.

My own company, Nucleus Software, is a highly focussed organisation. We consciously produced software only in banking sector and initially focussed on only one product.

The *mantra* is simple – focus on capturing a major market share in one product and then diversify.

Quality of your product or service: An entrepreneurial venture should produce quality products. There's a simple business logic behind this. You need to make every customer your sales person if you want to become the market leader. Your product should be such that your customer is not able to resist telling all his or her friends how good it is.

You will notice your sales force increasing with every passing day and slowly but surely you will capture the market share, just because your product is of superior quality.

Leadership plays an important role in entrepreneurship. An entrepreneur has to be a true leader to the team. Being a leader does not mean that you have the privilege to dominate your co-workers. A good leader always understands the problems and needs of team members and co-ordinates with them from time to time.

My friends and team members were the biggest inspiration for me. Whatever I have achieved till now is the result of their hard work and support. I started this company with two of my colleagues and today, we are a family of more than thousand members. I owe my success to my team members who consistently supported me.

I think that the *mantra* for success can be put in just four words—hard work, simplicity and humility.

Vishnu R. Dusad is the Managing Director of Nucleus Software. He is a veteran IT professional who is a source of inspiration to many. An individual with a rare combination of academic excellence, entrepreneurship and innovation, he is a graduate from the Indian Institute of Technology, New Delhi. He founded the Nucleus Workshop in 1984, following which Nucleus Software Exports was conceived in 1986. In 1994, Nucleus Software Solutions made its presence felt in Singapore. The following year saw Nucleus Software go public and was listed on the BSE.

Unicorn Books

Your résumé is your first introduction to the employer who has never seen you before. You need to give it the best shot to make the first winning move. The book 'Winning Résumé' fulfils this long-felt need for a contemporary guide on résumé writing that is in line with the expectations of global employers in this information technology driven age. The book breaks away from the traditional world of sequential cataloguing of degrees and job histories. Instead, it provides candidates seeking new jobs or job changes with contemporary techniques to fulfil a difficult task, to produce polished, subtle and refined advertisement-copy about their own selves.

Demy size • Pages: 136 • Price: Rs. 96/- • Postage: Rs. 15/-

This book's contents are far richer and deeper than other books on the subject. No contemporary book in the Indian market covers topics such as SWOT analysis, portfolio preparation, wardrobe tips, body language and interview preparation techniques that use question-and-answer sessions with analysis of top answers.

An exhaustive databank of frequently asked questions and model answers ensures you hold an advantage over other candidates. Finally, there's a bonus section containing tips on good résumé writing practices.

Sure Success in Interviews is a truly comprehensive, one-source guide that will turn you into a professional performer at any interview.

This book enables you to:

• How to write a winning résumé • Practical hints to overcome nervousness & boost confidence • SWOT (Strengths, Weaknesses, Opportunities & Threats) analysis • Portfolio preparation • Tips on wardrobe & self-grooming • Understanding body language • Interview preparation techniques through Q&A sessions • The art of successful follow-up.

Demy size • Pages: 156 • Price: Rs. 96/- • Postage: Rs. 15/-